MORAL LESSONS OF THE TWENTIETH CENTURY

MORAL LESSONS OF THE TWENTIETH CENTURY

Gorbachev and Ikeda on Buddhism and Communism

Mikhail Gorbachev
and
Daisaku Ikeda

Translated by Richard L. Gage

I.B. TAURIS
LONDON · NEW YORK

Published in 2005 by I.B. Tauris & Co Ltd
6 Salem Road, London W2 4BU
175 Fifth Avenue, New York NY 10010
www.ibtauris.com

In the United States of America and in Canada distributed by
Palgrave Macmillan, a division of St Martin's Press
175 Fifth Avenue, New York NY 10010

Copyright © Daisaku Ikeda and Mikhail Gorbachev, 2005
English Translation Copyright © Soka Gakkai, 2005

The right of Daisaku Ikeda and Mikhail Gorbachev to be identified as the authors of this work has
been asserted by them in accordance with the Copyright, Designs and Patents Act 1988.

All rights reserved. Except for brief quotations in a review, this book, or any part thereof, may not
be reproduced, stored in or introduced into a retrieval system, or transmitted, in any form or by
any means, electronic, mechanical, photocopying, recording or otherwise, without the prior written permission of the publisher.

ISBN 1 85043 975 3 (hardback)
EAN 978 1 85043 975 2 (hardback)
ISBN 1 85043 976 1 (paperback)
EAN 978 1 85043 976 9 (paperback)

A full CIP record for this book is available from the British Library
A full CIP record for this book is available from the Library of Congress

Library of Congress catalog card: available

Project management by M&M Publishing Services
Typeset in 11/12 pt Baskerville by FiSH Books, London
Printed and bound in Great Britain by MPG Books Ltd, Bodmin

Contents

Preface

This book is dedicated to the 20th century. Born during the fateful transitional period between the 1920s and 1930s, we have both experienced more than half the century and have produced this book as an investigation into the lessons it has left us.

We are of different cultural backgrounds and have engaged in different activities. One is a Russian raised in the Russian Orthodox culture; the other is a Japanese brought up in a Buddhist culture. One works through politics, the other works in the field of religion. It was no mere coincidence that brought us together in dialogue.

Our philosophies and articles of faith differ. One author was the last secretary general of the Communist Party of the Soviet Union. The other is the leader of the largest religious movement in Japan. For us to find a common spiritual basis enabling us to sit down at the discussion table and discover shared points through which we can understand the outstanding events of the 20th century has two consequences. First, it shows the significance of human experiences in the 20th century. Second, it proves that everyone living today—including the two of us, born and raised in different circumstances—has much in common.

The 20th century witnessed the oppressive ordeals of world conflicts and loathsome totalitarianism. At its close, the most pressing problems were those of values and freedom: that is, the right to live the lives granted us by heaven and nature, and the need to preserve the spirit of liberty and freedom of thought and faith.

The 20th was a century of fearsome ordeals from the standpoint of humanism. It exposed the venom in Promethean myths, the conceit of knowledge, and the lust to dominate Mother Nature.

This book attempts to see what lessons humanity can derive from the attempt to realize the ideals of socialist humanism, not only because one of the authors was a direct participant and witnessed the end of the great experiment, but also because the Soviet's practical application of socialist theory—striving for testing on a global scale—influenced the lives of people on practically every continent in the world.

We do not regard this period of socialist humanism as a black hole in history, because its egalitarian ideal made human beings more mature and wiser. We respect the socialist-humanist's romanticism and sense of mission. But socialist humanism failed, and its limitations and inconsistencies have been laid bare. Our dialogue takes its point of origin from the need for a new humanism with a new orientation. We are certain that the time has come for a true humanism that prizes the individual personality, protects the dignities and values of humanity, and avoids leading humanity into new temptations and catastrophes.

Twentieth-century experiences and warnings can provide grounds for the search for and construction of a 21st-century humanism. We start our speculative quest at the point where intolerant, extreme social-ist humanism and the dream of communist equality ended. We ask ourselves, if revolutionary extremism is dangerous, what kinds of social reform and development do we need? If ideological extremism defamed itself, how can we assure a sound foundation for faith and culture? If human happiness cannot be built on violence, how do we combat evil? Uniformity and egalitarianism applied to anything and everything brought destruction and damaged the diversity of life on earth. If this is the case, what must we do to ensure that the equal importance of each individual is reflected in reality, to protect human happiness and dignity, and to ensure equal rights to all? Since class ethics are incompatible with morality, what can we find to replace them? How can we guard the human dignity of people incapable of finding personal empowerment, a voice in the clamor of authority, or their own share of wealth and the good life?

Many pressing problems face former communist societies. In solving them we must protect the political and spiritual heritage of the new way of thinking and of the reforms and regeneration known as "perestroika" that put an end to the Cold War. How are we to go about this? What kind of world political system is going to replace the former bipolar system dominated by the Soviet Union and the United States?

All these questions are easier to pose than to answer. We know that there may yet be no answers to some of them and that old preconcep-tions and myths are not going to give place to new thinking and new humanism easily. Nonetheless, we are convinced that now is the time for broad global dialogue about the lessons we can learn from the 20th century and the nature of the new humanism and new values that can help humanity triumph over the tribulations of the post-communist period.

Mikhail S. Gorbachev
Daisaku Ikeda

CHAPTER ONE

Chance, Will, or Fate?

Ikeda: You and I are specialists in different fields—you in politics, I in Buddhism. In this dialogue, since our goal is to investigate the best ways for human beings to think and act, we must necessarily range far and wide over a spectrum of topics far exceeding our individual specialties. I hope the differences in our backgrounds and primary areas of experience and knowledge will intensify the interest of what we have to say. Most important of all, we must put what we have seen, done, and thought to good use for the sake of the youth of this new century.

Your appearance in the political arena in the 1980s was truly fateful for world history. Perestroika, of which you were the father, led to the end of the Cold War, the democratization of East Europe, and the downfall of the totalitarian communist regime in Russia. These events were sudden and totally unexpected. They changed the face of civilization and the fates of nations, ethnic groups, and individual human beings. They enriched humanity by the unique transformation of a communist totalitarian system into a democratic society.

Thinking about Perestroika today, when the historical scale of the transformations you initiated is making itself clearly felt, I often wonder how it all became possible. What personal qualities enabled you to undertake global democratic reforms? What would have happened to Russia—and to the world community—if, in 1985, you had not become general secretary of the Central Committee of the USSR?

In a speech you delivered at Soka University in April 1993, you partly answered these questions by saying, "The fate of each of us is inscrutable. We create our own lives. Nonetheless, each of us does have a destiny." When did you recognize your own fate and your historical mission? What do life, politics, fate, and history mean to you? Did you feel the influence of fate on your activities? What helped you overcome the apparently insuperable?

Gorbachev: My destiny was formed by my experience, by the things I lived through. It arose from a sense of responsibility. Indeed, for me, destiny and mission are synonymous with a sense of responsibility. All my actions were permeated by the belief that ethical democracy was possible in the former Soviet Union.

But democracy is incompatible with violence against individuals. Democracy devoid of morality is unacceptable. True democracy is impossible under conditions in which tanks fire on defenseless people and a whole nation is gripped by fear.

My generation—called the Sixty-somethings—strove almost instinctively for freedom and did everything possible to accelerate liberation from the Stalinist heritage. For me the Stalinist purges were no mere hearsay. My own grandfather was thrown into prison in 1937, and everyone in our village avoided us. Even neighbors ostracized us. I cast no blame on them. In those days, no one knew whose turn would come next. But the memories remain deep in my heart.

Many of us children of the Stalinist epoch were ignorant of the subtleties of liberalism. Still, we were highly zealous worshippers of freedom in everything, large and small. We strove for what we lacked: freedom of speech, discussion, and information. We dreamed of being able to determine our own fates.

Sooner or later, the Soviet people had to take account of their past, tell the truth about their sufferings, and pull the country together. This was their awakening to liberty. I am glad my like-thinkers and I—and not somebody else—were given the chance to break our country's standstill and begin democratic reforms.

Ikeda: The reforms were dramatic and might have been cataclysmic. But, as if by miracle, one of the greatest events of the 20th century took place with comparative tranquility and without the horrors that accompanied the collapse of Yugoslavia. Everyone agrees that the presence of Mikhail S. Gorbachev played a major part in minimizing the difficulties. Historians of the future will endorse Václav Havel's comment that Gorbachev assumed his post a typical bureaucrat and left it a true democrat.

One of your close associates, Alexander S. Tsipko, evaluates your political activities in his *Proshchanie s Kommunizmom* [Breaking with Communism]:

> No matter how paradoxical it seems at first glance, the fate of democracy in Russia depends much more on Gorbachev than on Yeltsin. I am not speaking of the current moment, but of democracy as a moral value, as a guideline for political development...As a personality and a human being, Gorbachev is connected with his reforms and with the future of democratic reforms in Russia. He stands at the source of our post-communist history. (Alexander S. Tsipko, *Komyunizumu tono Ketsubetsu* [Proshchanie s Kommunizmom], trans. Tsuneko Mochizuki [Tokyo: Simul Press, 1993], p.311)

Gorbachev: The soul of Bolshevism was leftist extremism. Though an a-political artist, the great Russian opera singer Feodor Chaliapin

(1873–1938) accurately describes it in *Maska i dusha* [Mask and Soul], his memoirs:

> In that combination of stupidity and cruelty—Sodom and Nebuchadnezzar—that is the Soviet regime, I see something fundamentally Russian. This is our native monstrosity in all its aspects, forms, and degrees... The trouble was that our Russian builders simply could not lower themselves to think about ordinary human beings in terms of a sensible, human-scale architectural plan. Instead, they absolutely had to raise a tower to the skies—a Tower of Babel. They could not be satisfied with the ordinary, healthy, bold stride with which a man walks to work and home again. They had to dash into the future with seven-league steps.
>
> 'Let's break with the past!' And all at once it becomes necessary to sweep away the whole world, leaving not a trace behind. And most important—all our Russian smart guys surprisingly know all about everything. They know how to turn a hunchback cobbler into a glorious, god-like Apollo. They know how to train a rabbit to light matches. They know what the rabbit needs to be happy. And they know what it will take to make the rabbit's offspring happy in two hundred years. (F. I. Shaliapin, *Maska i dusha: moi sorok let na teatrakh* [Moscow: V/O "Soiuzteatr" STD SSSR, 1991], p.222)

Actually, although they did not and could not know these things, their conviction that they did caused immense suffering.

Ikeda: And, once again, as has often happened in Russia, the peasantry suffered most cruelly. With your own peasant background, you fully understand their misery in, for instance, the agricultural collectivization of 1932. To the horror of the whole world, Bolshevik politicians created artificial famines that cost the lives of millions of peasants in the Ukraine, one of the great European grain-producing zones.

Gorbachev: Very true. The destruction of the peasants and their morality can be called one of the greatest evils perpetrated by the Bolsheviks.

Ikeda: In contrast to this Bolshevik mindset, by its nature Buddhism is not a teaching that an exalted being condescends to teach a lower being. It is based on ideas of equality, compassion, and symbiosis, according to which human beings are honest with each other and strive together for perfection. My own teacher Josei Toda, who had unique social talents and was second president of Soka Gakkai, revealed this to me.

In Buddhist philosophy, the highest being is a Buddha, who has attained inexhaustible wisdom, compassion, perspicacity, and the will to overcome difficulties. This being is, however, no deification capable of miracles and mystical actions. A Buddha is a human being filled with energy, the joy of life, and love for all living things.

Mahayana Buddhism teaches that each human being is innately capable of attaining the Buddha state. All people are absolutely equal. Discrimination on the basis of differences such as race is excluded. We can all develop and perfect ourselves to what we think are inaccessible heights. Differences make each individual unique, promote mutual spiritual enrichment, and diversify human society.

But the independent, unique individual must not wait for happiness to be bestowed. Mutual assistance and support consist not in foisting formulas for happiness on others, as even the most high-minded Bolsheviks wanted to do, but in cooperating in the discovery of the inexhaustible source of spiritual power within human beings.

Gorbachev: Certainly, we live in symbiosis with others and to a large extent are indebted to them—first of all to parents, spouses, and children. For much of my own success in life I am indebted to Moscow University. Its special atmosphere, respect for science, and concentration on students as well as the student friendships I formed there played a big role. I was the happiest man on earth when I first entered its sacred halls.

I am very critical of the simple reasoning that lays everything at destiny's door. We are guided most of all by interests, attractions, and the ideas and ideals of our time. We act within fixed frames of reference that are not easy to cross. Nothing begins with a blank page. I do not mean that everything in history happens in robot fashion. Even Marx, the materialist, recognized freedom of choice. Much more depends on us precisely because we are free. In its own turn, our inborn nature determines much in us.

Ikeda: The rapid current of time and unexpected events sometimes drastically alter our plans. In the pursuit of new destinies, we do things we once considered unacceptable. Obviously inherent in each of our lives are diverse life factors and a predisposition to various spheres of activity. But each of us also contains something stable—a spiritual system, a moral reaction, an absence of or an attraction to systematic education and culture. I think your driving life force has always been, first and foremost, a passion for enlightenment, the readiness to accept new knowledge and truths. The dogmatism of ignorance that sometimes compels politicians to commit acts of terror and cruelty is foreign to you. World history provides numerous examples of such cruelty. Robespierre and Lenin, two dogmatists absolutely certain of the soundness of their own ideas, opted for the use of terror. You, on the other hand, adopted the trial-and-error method, fully aware that you were the trailblazer and that your path was thorny and unexplored.

Gorbachev: In my life, as probably in yours, much has depended on chance. Looking back, I see that, from an early age, I was aware of a calling to social activity. When I was a boy, other children chose me to be their leader; they needed me. I worked with the Komsomol organization throughout my university days. Nonetheless, my fate might have turned out differently if, after graduation from Moscow State University in 1955, I had not gone home to Stavropol.

As a matter of fact, things were working out in favor of my remaining in Moscow. The university assignment committee had selected 12 graduates from the law faculty, including me, to work at the Office of the Public Prosecutor of the USSR. Rehabilitation of victims of Stalinist repression was in full swing and we 12 were going to work in newly organized departments verifying the legality of the ways state-security organs conducted their affairs. I envisioned my future work to be struggling for the triumph of justice, which coincided completely with my own political and moral convictions.

On June 30, returning to my dormitory after passing the final state examination, I discovered in my post box an official letter inviting me to my future workplace—the USSR Public Prosecutor's Office. I was expecting a discussion of my new duties. But when, elated and smiling, I crossed the threshold of the office indicated in the letter, a seated bureaucrat delivered the dry, official notification: "It is considered impossible to employ you in the organs of the USSR Public Prosecutor's Office." That was a real blow.

It seems that, only the night before, the government had issued a secret decree forbidding the recruiting of young law-school graduates to work in central organs of justice. It was claimed that one of the many reasons for the outburst of mass repression in the 1930s had been entrusting others' fates to green young people lacking professional and practical experience. As paradoxical as it sounds, I, a representative of a family that had suffered repression, became the unwilling victim of this new "struggle to establish socialist legality".

All my plans suddenly collapsed. Of course, I could have looked for a cozy place at the university to enable me to remain in Moscow. But, after considering and weighing everything, I decided to go back to the country.

Thanks to this occurrence, I discovered myself and set out on the right path towards achievements that are now independent of me. Was it all the result of chance, of fate?

Ikeda: For the most part, my youthful experiences were dominated by a reevaluation of the standards overturned by the Japanese defeat in World War II. Before the war, we had been forced to believe in the sanctity of imperial Japan and the emperor. Then, out of the blue, democracy replaced all that—with the assistance of the Occupation Forces. Bewildered by the drastic reorientation of official ideology, young people thirsted for spiritual support. I remember this period and the experiences associated with it very well. I longed to study but had to help our family. My father was seriously ill, and my older brothers had not yet returned from the front. I worked during the day and at night attended a trade school attached to the factory. Study materials were in short supply. We had to work literally in the dark because the electricity was constantly being turned off. I contracted tuberculosis. High temperatures and coughing up blood often kept me at home. Reading was my one pleasure. A group of young people my own age formed a book-lovers' club where we discussed philosophy and the books we were reading.

It was at this stage that I met the man who was to exert an enormous influence on the rest of my life. One hot summer evening, a friend from my elementary school days invited me to a philosophical discussion held at a private house where some 20 people had gathered. There, a man of about 40 was lecturing on the Buddhist teachings of the great Japanese priest Nichiren Daishonin. His simple, easy-to-understand, relaxed style of talking generated an inspirational atmosphere. That man was Josei Toda, who was to be my life teacher. Was it fate that brought us together? Maybe.

His forthright, trenchant answers to my questions convinced me that he could quench my thirst for knowledge and provide me with the key to truth. In discussing the teachings of Nichiren, he said: "The most important thing in the study of complex Buddhist philosophy is to grasp its essence through practical action. You must live according to the principles proposed by Nichiren, fundamentally improving your own life and helping others as you do so."

Toda was an extraordinary person. During the war, in spite of pressure from official Shintoism, he had staunchly maintained his Buddhist principles. For this, the militarists condemned him to two years' imprisonment. His courageous refusal to sacrifice his beliefs played the deciding role in my choosing him as a mentor.

My encounter with Mr Toda led me to accept the Buddhist faith. I became a Buddhist not because I immediately understood the essence of the teachings, but because this great humanist, so unlike ordinary religious leaders, evoked my profound trust and respect.

Before becoming a Buddhist, I had professed no religion. Our generation had been indoctrinated by official Shinto, thrust on us with the aim of raising military morale and national consciousness during World War II. From my youngest years, I had been forced to believe in the totalitarian ideology that, ultimately, led to national tragedy.

Religion ought to serve humanity and its happiness. But, as history and particularly Japanese experience show, faith is all too often manipulated to inculcate blind submission. Knowing this, I did not become a zealous believer all at once. At first, I was unable to rid myself of confusion and indecision. Moreover, I was seriously ill and uncertain whether I would have the strength to put humanistic Buddhist ideas to practical use. Doing so was, after all, a complicated task requiring enormous energy and endurance. But, gradually, from Mr Toda's teachings and my personal experience I came to understand that a certain law really does guide our lives and the universe, and that there is a religion revealing the essence of that law and leading to full harmony with it.

At the beginning of our conversation you said your destiny arose from your sense of responsibility. That sense transforms mere fortune into destiny. Buddhism finds what you call a strong sense of responsibility in a single moment in the individual's life (*ichinen*). The mighty efforts produced moment by moment by this prodigious will springing from each person's character, bringing forth a dramatic impact I call "human revolution", can transform a human personality and the world around that person.

Mahatma Gandhi demonstrated its power. The endurance and consistency with which he struggled for Indian independence astonished people. Nehru said that Gandhi removed the black pall of fear from the soul of the Indian people and transformed it entirely.

The French writer André Maurois (1885–1967) described the mighty history-changing potential inherent in individuals in *Au commencement était l'action* (Paris: Librarie Plon, 1966):

It is said that the true revolution is the revolution of a single person. More precisely, a single person, whether hero or saint, can set for the masses an example which when emulated will turn the planet over. (p. 93)

The great person of action does not follow the well-trodden path. Because he sees what others do not see, he does what others do not do. His will becomes a tidal wave that sweeps away habit and resistance. (p. 94)

Without Leonardo da Vinci, the Italian Renaissance would have been an empty dream. It is impossible to imagine the Russian spiritual renaissance of the first half of the 19th century without the name of Aleksandr S. Pushkin.

My point is not limited to the world of art. Buddhism teaches that "The example of a single person [who has attained Buddhahood] opens the way for all, because the same thing applies equally to all living beings. Social spiritual equilibrium and moral supports collapse without a person who sets the example for all others. Perhaps lack of such a person is the basic cause of the pathological condition of contemporary society."

Hegel calls the person who has penetrated the spirit of his age and created a new epoch the personification of the *Weltgeist*. The whole life of such a person is consumed with passion and struggle. Such a person never kowtows to authority and never becomes entangled in the desire for personal power.

Gorbachev: I agree to a point. Nonetheless, in determining individual destiny, I am disinclined to rely entirely on examples set by great individuals. It is rightly said that every age gives birth to its own heroes. Time, and not the snap judgments of contemporaries, delivers the verdict on an individual's service to history. There is, after all, an immense distance between the actions of great people and their consequences.

This reminds me of a book I obtained while still in senior classes at school. It contains literary-critical articles by the Russian writer Vissarion G. Belinsky (1811–48). Quoting Hegel on the heroism of the struggle and triumphing over hostile circumstances, Belinsky—a realist—keeps personality and dreams in the background and emphasizes reality. In an article on the play *Gore ot Uma* [Wit Works Woe] by Aleksandr S. Griboyedov (1795–1829), Belinsky issues a—to me, unforgettable—call for a steadfast perception of reality. This was extremely important to young people of my generation who were just crossing the threshold of home and setting out on journeys filled with many difficult trials.

I mean the kinds of difficulties that test their endurance. The true essence of a person, the person's real worth, becomes apparent not in days of triumph but in days of defeat. As is well known, life burns brightest in the battle with chaos, when the necessities of life are lacking, when everyone is against you, and you must start all over from nothing. I lived through such trials too.

In 1955, back in Stavropol after school, my wife and I lived in a single room in a one-story house on Staraya Kazanskaya Street. I shall never forget it. The tiny room was practically unfurnished. We had an iron coal-burning stove and an old iron bedstead. In the middle of the room, a big wooden box in which I had brought my books home from Moscow served as both table and bookshelf. We were lucky enough to have a couple of chairs too. We lived in that room for several years. Our daughter Irina was born there. But it was good that we started out from scratch in this way.

I have no regrets that the greater part of my young energy was expended in overcoming unfavorable circumstances. The hardships and daily adversities of the early years of my independence tempered me.

Things were hard for us, but we burned with the desire for a better, more interesting, and meaningful life. Past experience has taught me a very important lesson. Even in hard times and years of deprivation, human beings manifest what I would call normal human feelings. Probably the wisdom of life consists in being able to enjoy a festival, even when everything else looks dark.

Ikeda: Your experience proves that the difficulties and trials of youth temper the soul.

To return to my own young experiences, a year after my first meeting with Mr Toda I started working in his publishing company. Before the war, he had been a highly successful businessman with many diverse enterprises, including a private preparatory school where he continued his work as an educator. But all his holdings lost their value during his unjust wartime imprisonment, leaving him with immense debts.

After the war, he started a publishing company, where I edited a youth magazine *Boken Shonen* [Boy's Adventures]. I loved the work because, from my own childhood, I had dreamed of becoming a journalist and writing for a juvenile audience. I passionately wanted to make the magazine popular and conducted opinion polls in schools to investigate reader preferences. But the difficult macroeconomic situation and our own shortage of funds forced us to discontinue publication.

Mr Toda also headed a credit cooperative, to which I was transferred. But, as it was barely scraping along, the majority of my fellow workers started looking for other jobs.

Finally, in spite of all efforts to save it, the credit cooperative, too, went bankrupt. We were up to our ears in debt. Threatening creditors dunned us every day. First our salaries were delayed; then they were cut in half. Finally they stopped altogether. Employees resigned, and Mr Toda was left with only me and two or three helpers.

At about that time, I moved out of my parents' home and rented a small room. Things were very bad. Even in winter, I went without an overcoat. My trousers were in tatters and my socks darned somehow or another. A cough tortured me constantly, and fever exhausted me.

Even in the face of total business failure, my relationship with Mr Toda remained unaltered. Calm and self-reliant in the darkest hours, he used to say: "Defeats on the long road of life don't mean the life itself has been a failure." I was willing to share all hardships with him to the end, though my doctors said I probably would live to be no more than 30. Still I tried to be optimistic.

The period leading up to the liquidation of Mr Toda's credit cooperative was for me both the hardest and the happiest. My heavy load of work compelled me to give up the night classes I had enrolled in. But Mr Toda gave me personal instruction. On all our days off and before work on ordinary days he sacrificed his own rest to teach me political science, economics, law, literature, physics, and so on. Concentrated essences of knowledge, the lectures of this erudite man were my university.

Origins and Traditions Manifest Themselves in Us

Ikeda: Several persons who know you well say that your hometown, Stavropol, contains a key to the secret of how a man like Mikhail S. Gorbachev appeared in the Kremlin. The magnificent peaks, mountain valleys and pastures, and gently delineated hills of the Caucasus, where Stavropol is located, have attracted me since childhood, when I was engrossed in Lev Tolstoy's stories of the region.

The Caucasus, including Stavropol, has a long tradition of independence. It had its own government without police or bureaucrats for about 300 years. Growing up in such a region, you can never have found democracy alien. It is an integral part of the history of the Caucasus.

Traditions and childhood environment reflect in a person's character and way of life. In Japan, Russia, and everywhere else, where we are born leaves a stamp on our mind cast.

How did the democratic traditions of Stavropol and the Caucasus influence you as a politician?

Gorbachev: It is difficult to explain why a person is one kind of a human being and not another, why some have an inclination for freedom and truth that others lack. Researchers often speak of my home region as belonging to a special South Russian type. They say that natives of the Northern Caucasus are more openhearted. I would not say that the residents of the North Caucasus are more democratic by nature than, for instance, the Russians of Pskov or Novgorod. In these republics, government was conducted by what is called a *veche*, a popular assembly, similar to the New England Town Meetings that Emerson said were a vital part of American democracy. The Pskov and Novgorod systems have made a substantial contribution to the world treasury of democratic institutions.

The indigenous peoples of the Caucasus, however, were characterized by cruelty, especially in battle. They staunchly supported the tsarist regime.

As time passed, the Caucasus became an important line of defense for Russia. Forts were built—Stavropol was one of them—and the region was colonized. Peasants from outside—among them my ancestors—wcre forcibly transported to the Caucasus. I am not certain whether I should be called Russian or Ukrainian. My mother was a Ukrainian, with the typically Ukrainian name of Gopkalo. Her ancestors were from the Chernigov region. My paternal great-grandfather was a native of the province of Voronezh.

Ikeda: In his story *Hadji Murat*, a drama of a non-Russian and a Muslim living in the Caucasus, Tolstoy's attitude toward his hero is impartial and magnanimous. Of course, he was an exceptional person. Still, generosity toward other people seems characteristic of many Russians.

Gorbachev: In the past, people paid less attention to ethnic background. At the 1991 conference in the Belavezheskaja forests, Russia, the Ukraine, and Belarus established the Commonwealth of Independent States, thus dismantling the Soviet Union. Only after this tragic turn in events did people start concerning themselves with bloodlines, that is, whether someone is a "pure" Ukrainian or a "pure" Russian. For our ancestors—like my grandparents—being Russian meant something entirely different. It meant belonging to the unified Russian nation, to the Orthodox religion, and to Russian culture. No one paid much attention to whether a person was a *khokhol* (Ukrainian) or a *katsap* (Russian). It is not surprising then that from childhood everyone in Stavropol or along the Kuban River knew both Ukrainian and Russian songs and switched easily from one language to the other.

The people of our region are sociable and inclined to compromise since, for the nations of the Northern Caucasus, agreement has long been a major means of survival. As a result of mind cast and the nature of our interpersonal relations, we were fated to be internationalists.

Ikeda: Harmonious coexistence of peoples of various ethnic backgrounds and common cultural and historical conditions usually cultivate an internationalist frame of mind.

In addition to being an initiator of educational reform, the first president of Soka Gakkai, Tsunesaburo Makiguchi, was an outstanding scientific geographer. In his great work *A Geography of Human Life*, published in 1903, on the basis of materials related to his own home region, he painstakingly researched diverse mutual relations between human beings and their environment. In the introduction to the book, he wrote: "every aspect of the entire universe can be found in the small, limited area of one's home community. But we have to be sensitive to these unfolding riches all around us, and we must learn how to be effective observers."

Mr Makiguchi subtly noted the influences the environment—natural and climatic conditions—has on a person's character, way of thinking, and lifestyle. Geography influences not only local regions, but also ethnically based nations. All members of each nation share a common identity, of which there are at least as many as there are ethnic groups. Keeping the peace in large aggregates of such groups can be hard, as the example of the highly heterogeneous Soviet Union showed.

Gorbachev: Unfortunately, because of Soviet dogmatism and economic determinism, we—and all our social sciences—gave little thought to the influence of geographic factors on the human psyche and disposition. Mr Makiguchi's work includes many correct observations. It is true that people living in sunny climates have sunnier dispositions.

After spring floods, a river leaves behind many large and small pools. In a similar way, over the centuries, population movements and migrations have left behind many highly diverse ethnological groups around Stavropol. Few regions of the world have experienced so much linguistic, cultural, and religious contiguity within so compact a territory.

Our multinational, multilingual, multifaceted environment has taught us many things, the most important of which are tolerance, delicacy, and mutual respect. To offend or insult a Caucasian mountaineer was to make a deadly enemy. To respect his worth and customs, on the other hand, was to win the most faithful of friends. I had many such friends because in my young days, though still ignorant of the theoretical basis for my conviction, I gradually came to see that tolerance and concord, not enmity, are the ways to create peace among peoples.

Later, when I became president of the USSR and found myself confronted with the problems of nations, I was no novice at dealing with such issues. Here, too, I found the sources of my own inclination to seek compromise in the spiritual culture of the Northern Caucasus.

That culture does not, as is sometimes thought, represent weakness of character. There have been bold mutineer types enough in the

Northern Caucasus. It is not by accident that the leaders of many genuinely popular movements of the 17th and 18th centuries—for instance, Kondraty Bulavin and Ignat Nekrasov, Stepan (Stenka) Razin, and Emelian Pugachev—marshaled their forces and began their campaigns in the Caucasus. According to tradition, the subjugator of Siberia, Yermak Timofeyevich, too, was from our part of the country.

Still, by and large, southern Russians are innately open-minded and mild. Though no angels, they do not pick fights. They smile a lot and love and enjoy life.

Ikeda: The ethnic and cultural diversity of your background helped make you the kind of citizen of world society—a true internationalist—that the 21st century needs.

The Tragedy of War and the Philosophy of Peace

Ikeda: A strikingly youthful atmosphere, quite unlike the stereotyped image of the place, pervaded the Kremlin when I first met you there in July 1990. Chingiz Aitmatov was present at the time; and, pointing to him and smiling, you called him your close friend. I was pleased to note amity between a great politician and a great writer. On that occasion, our free exchange of opinions and the prevailing intellectual atmosphere produced on me an impression of springtime freshness. I felt as if the harmonious thoughts and feelings of survivors of the long Soviet winter and harbingers of spring were about to strike responsive chords in me.

The spiritual potential of our mature years is accumulated in youth. In spite of the furnace of trials it has passed through, your soul no doubt still preserves riches obtained in youth in the form of loyalty to friends. What youthful encounters remain dear to you now? What are your ideas about the role of youth in later life?

Gorbachev: The lessons-in-life and the fates of people born in the 1930s have much to teach. The sufferings, hardships, and deprivations we knew did not make for a pleasant environment. Suffering may be ennobling, but being happy does not always require living a life of suffering and deprivation as we did in wartime. Nor do we require as a prerequisite for a happy later life the spiritual experiences of Stalinism and post-Stalinism. This was a time when, instinctively, we strove to undervalue our own opinions, to silence our own voices, and to conform in ways that reduce the soul to ashes. No one wanted to—we may even have been afraid to—be accused of insufficient loyalty to the authorities or the Party line.

Nonetheless, even during the Stalinist period, we had characteristic youthful hope. We made friends and trusted them. These were all manifestations of natural human emotions. Furthermore, conscience, moral criteria, and devotion preserved their influences as values and as reference points for human behavior.

We were wartime children who survived. Nothing of the life and deeds of our generation is understandable unless we take this into consideration. Because we shouldered the responsibility for our families' survival and for our own subsistence, we little boys became instant grownups. Peace, and with it our ordinary lives, collapsed before our eyes. The breakdown immediately transported us from childhood to adulthood. As children will, we went on enjoying life. We played hide-and-seek and ball games. But somehow we objectively watched ourselves playing. And we watched with adult eyes.

Probably our early experiences explain why we wartime children decided to change our way of living and to break once and for all with Stalinist socialism.

Ikeda: "Wartime children." Those words express the sufferings and deprivations that unite our generation. As you say, the new generation will open a new era, leaving behind the old systems that produced the tragedies of war. Still, humanity must not forget what war is. Our inescapable debt is to relate to future generations the full weight of the suffering war brings.

I first experienced the horror of an air raid when I was seventeen. We children had just been evacuated to an aunt's house. Our parents were to join us the next day. The bombing started that night. When an incendiary bomb hit it, my aunt's house burst into a sea of fire. My little brother and I barely managed to jump from the flames. The whole house burned to the ground. To this day I recall my fear as I watched the red glare against the night sky.

My four elder brothers had already been drafted and I, the fifth son and the oldest still at home, had to take care of my family while suffering from pulmonary tuberculosis.

As I have already said, Japanese children then were subjected to martial indoctrination. We were taught that serving the emperor and the government gave our lives true meaning. As a mere teenager, I believed in the sacredness of my military debt to the fatherland and wanted to join a youth air corps. A naval officer brought my application to our house for my father's approval. But he refused categorically to give it. He already had four sons at the front and would not allow his fifth to join up. The officer understood his objection; and I did not join the military. Although as an adult I have always been grateful to my father, I was bitterly disappointed at the time. My own young experiences bear witness to the mighty, total, and pernicious influence the military education of those years exerted on childish souls. Memories of them still agitate me.

After leaving school, I worked at a steel mill where ordinary instruction was combined with military training conducted in a building on the mill grounds. At first we produced finishing items for large ships. Then, when the mill started taking military orders, we built one-man torpedo boats. These boats had enough fuel only for the outward run. When they struck enemy craft, they and their target blew up together. The duty of the patriot was to perform deadly tasks for the good of the state willingly. The famous kamikaze pilots performed such a duty.

In May 1946, we received word of my eldest brother's death on the Burma front. I still react emotionally to the memory of my mother's mournful, defenseless look. Generally she was a strong person, but this blow seemed to stun her.

My own reaction was to question our reasons for going to war in the first place. In my youth I was indignant at the senseless tragedy and cruelty. I knew that, in the final analyses, the false patriotism our leaders propounded could lead only to war. When, at the age of nineteen, I first met him, feelings of this kind prompted me to ask Josei Toda about the nature of a true patriot.

Everything I now do in the name of peace derives from the tragic element in my wartime experiences and thoughts.

I chose to start my novel, *The Human Revolution*, in Okinawa, Japan's hardest-hit prefecture in the war years. I wrote: "War is barbarous and inhuman. Nothing is more cruel, nothing more tragic."

Gorbachev: Peace means struggling against forgetting. The war remains a world apart, deep in our recollections. Like you, my own responsibilities grew greatly after my father went to the front. People did their utmost for the "war effort" and for "victory". Mother worked on a collective farm from morning to night. This meant that I had to grow food for us to eat. All the other farmers lived under the same conditions until the end of the war.

In late 1942, thousands of displaced civilians and Soviet Army troops passed through our village.

Ikeda: Fleeing from the Nazis?

Gorbachev: Yes. The majority were women, children, and old people.

15

In a daze after having lost loved ones, they were barely able to drag themselves along. The despondent soldiers knew the Fascists were not far behind. Words like "ruin" and "failure" always call to mind the fires burning on the horizon and the sorrowful, suffering looks on the faces of those evacuees.

Nor could our family expect anything good from the Nazis. As the head of a collective farm, my grandfather was in danger of being shot. He packed his belongings and fled.

Passing through in their turn, the Germans left behind a garrison that employed local soldiers who had run away from the front and had been in hiding for months. My village, called Privol'noe, was occupied from August 3, 1942 until January 21, 1943.

The Germans also recruited local villagers to be what they called *Polizei*, to harass their fellows and dispatch them to forced labor. My mother was forced to work and often said that the *Polizei* stationed nearby, some members having been recruited from the villages, were most dangerous to the local people. Many of our people faced the firing squad, and we heard rumors of gassings. The rumors were later confirmed.

When word got out that the Germans were planning to punish houses where Communist Party members lived, my mother and my paternal grandfather sent me to hide on a farm about thirty kilometers away. It was probably the German defeat at Stalingrad that saved us.

Memories of the war continue to disturb and worry and to demand action. These are not mere empty phrases. And I consider the experiences of our men and women on the front during the Great War for the Fatherland very close to my heart.

I was just past ten years old when the war started. At that age, though we may not understand it all, we perceive everything. Even now I seem to see the village meeting where, standing, we listened to a speech by Molotov about the fascist Germany's treacherous aggression. In a few weeks, the young men had all gone to the front, leaving behind the old, the women, and the children. Soon village homes were receiving word of battle deaths of fellow villagers. I witnessed the grief and desperation of widowed women and of mothers who lost their sons. I know how hard life was for them thereafter. I know how war robbed them of their paramount joys: family, love, and friendship. That was—and remains— a calamity and a great sorrow for millions of people. The war left very few families unscathed.

I can still see thousands of people fleeing from fascist attacks, abandoning their homes and their work, losing their friends and near relations. We endured the horrible sight of our troops' retreat in the summer of 1942—and the German occupation. We witnessed treachery and desertion among Soviet soldiers, and reprisals on the part of the fascists. How bitterly we grieved at each Soviet defeat, and how we rejoiced at Soviet victories near Moscow and later at Kurskaya Duga near Stalingrad.

When I first traveled to Moscow after middle school, I saw how war had destroyed cities like Rostov, Kharkov, Voronezh, Kursk, and, of course, Stalingrad. But, like everyone else, I rejoiced at the revival of our country.

Given the ability to perceive the pain and the joy of the times, participating in events like these inevitably leaves profound traces in the soul and may determine one's choice in life and one's deeds. Like readiness to resist hardships, courage is not born of itself. It is the result of overcoming both one's own weaknesses and real obstacles.

Ikeda: That is why I am concerned about the fate of generations today who have grown up in a world of plenty, isolated from the misfortunes and sufferings that befell the generations of the war and the immediate postwar period. We must be grateful that they have escaped what we endured and that they are ignorant of the burdens of disorder and poverty. But, one way or another, the piper must be paid. The person who has never suffered is unlikely to empathize with the sufferings of others. He may even be capable of ignoring others' misfortunes. There are no rules governing reactions. The humiliated and impoverished sometimes grow hardhearted. Still, suffering opens the heart to people and the eyes to things the well-fed generally overlook.

Experience of suffering and humiliation made Fyodor Mikhailovich Dostoyevsky one of the most psychologically profound writers of world literature. In his case, ten years of penal servitude gave birth to one of humankind's geniuses.

People today think about the soul and the existence of things more important than satiety and comfort only when reminded of the horror of death and the transience of life.

Gorbachev: When we met at the Kremlin in 1990, Perestroika was accelerating and clearly had become irreversible. As you said, we were experiencing a springtime of change. We lived on that festival of freedom, on the awareness that our plans were coming true. We were happy to be witnesses, participants, and creators of a new, free country.

But the coin has another side too. As well as savoring the joys of spring, one must meet the autumn of defeat courageously. When this is necessary we can find strength in the adversities of youth and the tenacity with which we stood our ground in times of breakdown and trial.

This is especially important for young people dreaming of becoming politicians and of preparing themselves for political struggle. Aspiring politicians must, above all, have an immovable inner core—something incorruptible no matter how their careers develop—and be sure of families, close associates, and friends. This firm sense of self is the alpha and omega of a politician's success.

Ikeda: Your comment on self-sufficiency takes me back to the topic of youth. In today's comfortable world, becoming an individual—finding one's own *I*—is more complicated than it was in our time. It is hard for a young person today. To achieve something, he must work hard on preparing himself and be ready for competitive struggle. Easy, comfortable conditions at the start of life often fail to provide possibilities for realizing the value—the pricelessness—of one's *I* or to comprehend a solicitous relation to one's self and one's life. I cannot understand the psychology of drug addicts: they consciously kill themselves. How and when are we to cultivate self-esteem, respect for one's own *I* and its worth? Under contemporary conditions, the problem of the *I* is different and no doubt demands different approaches.

Gorbachev: I should like to make another observation based on Soviet history about the danger of maximalism; that is, of revolutionary extremism.

Extremism is as tenacious as the seduction of easy solutions. In the 20th century, countless people suffered because of the naïve belief in miraculous one-stroke solutions to all difficulties. In each new generation there are always radicals calling for a complete break with the past, a profound upheaval. Such people believe that the greater the destruction of the past, the greater the hope that the future will flourish.

That is all nonsense and deception. Deep roots in the past make the new durable. Only gradual, evolutional reforms ensure the irreversibility of change. The 19th- and 20th-century conviction that the most radical, the most revolutionary acts guarantee the endurance of change and progress was false. We can now say that evolutionary development and gradual reform consonant with the nature of humanity and social life are more effective than the revolutionary quest.

Although we learned important things from the 20th century, we have not found the whole truth. In many instances, the wisdom of the future must be founded on the wisdom of the past.

Ikeda: My belief and long-standing convictions are in moderation and the principles of gradual change. You were brought up on the highly radical ideology of Bolshevism. It is surprising, therefore, that you insisted on the importance of gradual reform and development. Though to some they seem fossils, in fact the principles of the gradual and moderate embody profound human wisdom.

Of course, mere slowness does not represent the principle of gradualness. Physical speed is not the issue. The essential thing is for development to be both gradual and, first and foremost, in the best interests of humanity. Reforms, progress, and development must be made for the sake, not at the cost, of human happiness. Developers must not limit their sights to their own aims or strive blindly to achieve given results without taking human well-being into consideration. We must remember that everything must be done for humanity. This is my understanding of the principle of gradualness.

The principle of gradualness is brilliantly illustrated by Shakyamuni's method of teaching as described in the Lotus Sutra. Conscious of the imperative need to make widely available the truth he himself had attained, Shakyamuni taught that the road to Enlightenment is open to everyone. This means that each individual human being is of priceless importance. Many people are accustomed to thinking of beings like the Buddha or God as abiding in some distant place, inaccessible to ordinary mortals. Unable to divest themselves of such preconceptions, Shakyamuni's audience found his idea startling and hard to understand. At first, Shakyamuni gives them a theoretical explanation. Since only one person in the audience understood, he moves on to parables through which he hoped to convince those who could not or would not grasp the essence of his message.

One of those parables is the celebrated tale of the Burning House. In it, some children—representative of all humanity—are so absorbed in games that they fail to notice that their large old house is engulfed in flames. Their father (Shakyamuni) calls them to come out, but they prefer to go on playing. After thinking a while, the father invites them for a ride in a huge, wonderful cart (the Teaching) that has drawn up at the door. Delighted the children rush out, each striving to be the first to board the magnificent vehicle. In this way the father saves his foolish children from the fire.

Sensing Shakyamuni's great love, his listeners sincerely longed to understand. Shakyamuni therefore continued by telling them that he and they are bound by profound ties existing since distant, previous lives. He said: "You may have forgotten; but I remember. You were close to me then and remain close to me now. You have once again gathered round me to understand the truth of life. Is that not so?"

As a result of this step-by-step approach, those who formerly could not grasp the idea of universally accessible Buddhahood gradually came to comprehend. Ashamed of their ignorance, his disciples vowed to accept the teaching and to guard and respect all life: their own and those of others as well.

Thus Shakyamuni, the Enlightened One, strove to lead people to understand, accept, and enthusiastically practice his philosophy of self-perfection. He did not compel. He did not condescend. Nor did he speak for his own enjoyment, ignoring the inability of people to understand the essence of his teaching. His soul was constantly troubled to find a way to transmit the truth that enables them to enter the orbit of happiness. Skillful use of parables and persuasion are the hallmarks of the compassionate and gradual method he employed to achieve this aim.

In connection with your comments on radicalism and extremism, I might say that nothing—not even scientific ideas—instilled in human consciousness by means of violence endures. Contemporary radicalism falls into the trap of mistaking knowledge for wisdom. Certainly, human knowledge has grown incredibly in many areas. Knowledge alone, however, does not necessarily bring wisdom. Indeed, wisdom is not infrequently inversely proportional to knowledge. It can be said that, when bloated and arrogant, knowledge desiccates wisdom. Contemporary radicalism errs by equating the two and trying to force social change according to plans compiled solely on the basis of knowledge. Advocates of this ideology think that the faster recognized goals are attained, the better. They also think it is permissible to use force to compel others to see eye to eye with them. Such radicalism has spilled seas of blood and caused untold suffering.

Gorbachev: Struggle and conflicts burn up the diversity of life, leaving only a social desert behind. Today, a caring attitude toward Nature presupposes a solicitous and caring attitude toward humanity, with all its inherent passions and contradictions of worth and weakness. This means getting to know humanity in order to live in harmony with ourselves, to control ourselves, and to perfect our volition. We must not seek to destroy or remake or to demand the impossible of humanity. The idea of the omnipotent god-man endowed with all rights is extremely dangerous and can be fatal.

On the basis of our post-communist experience, we in Russia have become convinced that radicalism and revolutionary extremism can assume the most unexpected and cynical forms. Violence against what is owned by society is just as pernicious as destruction of what belongs to the individual. In both instances, the human being is the victim. This is why the struggle with the philosophy of violence is always topical.

CHAPTER TWO

Perestroika and Freedom

Ikeda: In 1990, you told me that the main significance of Perestroika is the freedom it brought. In thinking about how freedom is put to use, you cited an example that recalls a Platonic allegory. The rays of the sun blind a person who suddenly emerges into the light after long confinement in a dark prison or a deep well. Similarly, people who have suddenly received freedom use their newly acquired independence solely to dwell on the past instead of examining the present and thinking about the future.

You, of course, sincerely believe in Perestroika, as is shown in a letter written to me by Chingiz Aitmatov. I received this letter, which bears the title "A Parable Related to Gorbachev", soon after you retired from the presidency.

In the Kremlin.

That meeting stands out in my mind more than all others. I assume that Gorbachev summoned me with a concrete aim, most probably, as I now think, to discuss the pressing situation in Middle Asia, particularly the national crisis. But, perhaps because of my own unintentional fault, instead of concerning substantial business, our conversation took an entirely different turn. This is why.

To understand the heart of what happened, the reader must realize that Perestroika as a process of unprecedented democratic reforms was in full swing. But a subterranean rumble of dissatisfaction and ever-rising criticism was distinctly gathering momentum from the right and the left—from the democrats and the bureaucrats. Everyone had his own arguments and reasons. The national economy was steadily sinking.

Certainly Gorbachev's mind was uneasy at that hour. Although the imprint of inner anxiety lay on his face, he controlled himself as usual. When he smiled cordially, his eyes occasionally flashed with the characteristic Gorbachev sparkle.

We were seated across from each other at a desk in one of his Kremlin offices. In a natural fashion, before getting down to the main topic, Gorbachev demonstrated interest in my literary affairs—what was new, what was I working on, could he expect a novel or a short story? Soon? Without realizing it, he touched on a very tender topic. In those days, I had practically no time for literary worry. I decided to tell him all about it.

'Well, how can I put it, Mikhail Sergeyevich?' I answered. 'It's getting harder and harder to write. We seem to have won our complete freedom, but we get far fewer results. There's no time left over at all. We're all caught up in Perestroika. All of us are being tossed by the same wind.'

'More like seven winds', smiled my Gorbachev.

'You're right', I agreed. 'Perstroika's got us running around in circles. I had no idea democracy would devour time this way.'

'I understand, I really do,' Gorbachev said thoughtfully with a sympathetic smile. 'Of course there's not enough time. But we have won something very important for the soul. In these days, we scarcely have time for a minute's thought. And everybody— every artist, philosopher, politician, and man in the street—has something to say.'

During the subsequent conversation I broached a problem that the socialist ideo- logical pall had long concealed and that was very much on my mind. It was the issue of the fatality of power for its wielder—a fatality arising from the eternally contradic- tory and therefore inevitably catastrophic nature of power itself. I had a premonition that this fatal question would, to one extent or another, affect the destiny of Gorbachev himself.

He had set forth on the path of a still not universally recognized reformer-martyr under totalitarian conditions. In short, we talked about the phenomenon of power and about the means and aims of dominion by one person over many. But, since the head- on approach would have been tactless, I took the long way round. In speaking of my own creative plans, I introduced a certain oriental fable, which was the key element in one of my future themes. I related it to him as if thinking aloud.

I said a certain story—an ancient tale—stuck in my mind. I thought about it while driving from place to place, at meetings, alone, and in a crowd. This is how it goes.

Once a certain prophet or soothsayer and a great lord engaged in a confidential and exceedingly frank conversation. The guest said to the lord, 'Your fame is wide- spread. You sit firmly on your throne. But I have heard an apparently odd rumor that you dream of doing your people a long-lasting favor by pointing the way to general happiness. In fact, you dream of giving them complete freedom and equality.' 'Yes', replied the lord, 'I have long been incubating such ideas and actually intend to do as you say. Such is my conviction and decision.'

Silent for a few moments, the wise guest said, 'Sire, so great a wish for the good of many does you undying honor and raises your image to the level of the gods. With all my heart, I am on your side. But it is my duty to tell you the whole truth. After hear- ing what I have to say, you must choose. Sire, you have two ways, two fates, two possibilities and are free to act as you deem necessary. One way to rule is to govern strictly in order to strengthen your throne following the traditions of your forebears. You are now at the pinnacle of your rightful, hereditary, stable power. You are strong and mighty. If you choose this first way of ruling you will remain on the same path and wield power to the end of your days. You will live for your own good and that of your people, and your heirs will follow in your footprints.'

Gorbachev remained silent and concentrated on my words. My parable was fairly transparent and less than gripping, since it dealt with distant, fabulous times.

Next I related the second choice set forth in the traveler's prediction. 'The second fate of a man at the peak of power is the difficult path of martyrdom. You must know, master, that its recipients will transform the freedom you give them into black ingrati- tude. That is the nature of such phenomena. And why? Why should such absurdity, such illogicality prevail? It ought to be the other way around. Where is the justice, the sense, in this situation? No one can say. Such is the inscrutable secret of heaven and the netherworld. Such is the way it has always been and will always be. And such will be your lot too.

'Once liberated, the people will become disobedient and will take vengeance on you for their past. They will abuse you in the crowds, revile you in the bazaars, and scoff and mock you and those close to you. Many of your trusted comrades-in-arms will be openly impertinent to you and misconstrue your instructions. And you will know, O great one, grief and humiliation to the end of your days and will never escape even your close associates' lust to drag you from your place and trample your name underfoot.

'Thus, Mighty Lord, you may choose between these two fates.' The lord replied, 'Wait seven days. I will summon you. Depart now, and go your way.'

This is the old story I told Gorbachev. He sat silent. The look on his face changed. Beginning to regret what I had done, I prepared to say goodbye and go when he said with a bitter smile, 'I know what you're talking about. But there's no need to wait for seven days—not even seven minutes. I have already chosen. No matter what it costs me, no matter how my fate turns out, I'll hold to my course. Democracy, freedom, deliverance from the fearsome past, and no dictatorship over anybody—these are the only way. And the people can judge me however they like. I am ready to follow that path, even if many of my contemporaries fail to understand me.'

With that we parted.

Gorbachev: And I now repeat the words I said to my friend Chingiz Aitmatov then: democracy and freedom alone. I have stuck to that and always will. I regret nothing. The country is now on the way to democratic transformation. That was my most significant achievement.

Young Russian democracy is going through a difficult period. The question of a democratic alternative to authoritarianism and the regime of personal power is once again pressing. Not merely political, the conflict involves value criteria and world outlooks. The autocratic idea is in opposition to faith in the ability of the peoples of Russia to continue on the path of independent development. The drama of the situation is that the very people who, three or four years ago, threatened the center in the name of freedom and democracy later became confirmed advocates of the absolute power of the president to rule with an iron hand. Nothing could be more monstrous and unnatural than Russian democratic supporters of autocracy.

No one can say that Russia today is a democratic nation in the true meaning of the words. The events of October 3 and 4, 1993 scorched the seedlings of democracy that we planted. That was literally a catastrophe. Crushed was the burgeoning belief that we Russians are forever finished with civil war and that we can resolve conflicts peacefully, without resorting to force. When all is said and done, the events of 1993 degraded us as citizens.

But take note of this. Even after everything that happened, the ruling regime could not turn the nation back. Immediately after the events of October 3 and 4, outstanding representatives of the democratic intelligentsia—former dissidents including Mikhail Gefter, Andrei Sinyavsky, Vladimir Maksimov, Petr Egides, and Gleb Pavlovskiy—said a resounding "no" to firing canons at the legally elected parliament. This kind of thing helped the nation recover from shock and shake off fear.

Interestingly, the reaction began to fade a few days after the tragedy. Conditions were created for holding parliamentary elections on December 12. The people voted against violent, radical revolution from above and against shock therapy. They demonstrated distrust of the politicians who had deliberately provoked the armed confrontation in Moscow in October 1993.

Only ten years earlier, few people believed we Russians would ever hold free, multiparty elections. But we did. The dream of all Russian democrats came true. Still, to my great concern, a recoil away from democracy occurred and is continuing.

Ikeda: Frankly, many people in Japan were surprised by what happened in Russia after your retirement. When you became general secretary in 1985, we were pleased that a young, charming, affable person had become leader of the USSR. Everyone began to expect great things of you. But no one thought the reforms you started would go as far as they did. Your policy of Glasnost led to the abolition of censorship and to freedom of emigration, speech, and religion. Political prisoners were released. The democratic revolution from above that you conceived changed the spiritual climate of Russia.

But, to tell the truth, many Japanese intellectuals are disappointed by later spiritual processes in Russia. Moral initiatives falter. Moral issues are excluded from reforms, especially economic reforms. Apathy and disappointment in democracy replace the enthusiasm evoked by Perestroika and the first free elections. More and more people are losing faith in politics and politicians. Alienation has replaced the general fervor that swept everybody up at the beginning of Perestroika. On a recent trip to Russia, a certain observer said to me: "Russians—especially Muscovites—are tired of contemporary politics and preaching."

At one time, the printed word was creative enough to shatter the hard ground of the past. But no one believes in the word any more. Perhaps negative reactions are bound to follow political upsurges. Maybe that is revolutionary logic. But the withdrawal of youth from politics and a growing social political apathy are ominous. I think it was Thomas Mann who said a people who despise politics always have despicable politics. Totalitarianism in either its left or right variant rushes in to fill a spiritual vacuum.

Gorbachev: Your analysis of the situation seems correct. We are moving from the stage of the political activity of abrupt change to a state of apathy. I am especially disturbed to see many people trying to portray indifference as a sign of stability. You are correct in saying that some among us wish to use stability to justify a tendency to authoritarianism.

All opinion polls show that the people do not want to go back. They are in favor of democratic reforms. Russia is capable of mastering democratic institutions and using them to reform the country. As they undertake political reforms they are simultaneously creating a civil society. Foundations, associations, clubs, parties and movements of all kinds, formerly totally unknown to us, are springing up. I am convinced that Russia will definitely become a democratic nation. We had to take risks for freedom. It was worth it, even though it meant losing power.

You insist that we politicians look on our lives and works with the eyes of eternity. I suggest a simpler idea: we look at ourselves and our deeds through the eyes of our children and grandchildren. Truthfully, when I look into the eyes of my friends and close associates, I have nothing to be ashamed of.

Russian young people today are open and free in their judgments. All of world culture is accessible to them. But, until Perestroika, we had the strictest kind of censorship. Even analysis—not to mention criticism— of Marxism-Leninism was forbidden. Pre-Revolutionary idealistic philosophy was prohibited, as was emigrant literature. Solzhenytsin and common sense were both outlawed. Yet, in the course of a few years, all these prohibitions have vanished. Glasnost was a true democratic revolution, a revolution of the soul.

What would my fate have been if I had chosen the beaten path? Power and nothing else? Enjoyment of special privileges? None of that interested me. I had observed it all at close range during the Brezhnev period. Most important of all, I came to power when repeating old experiences had become unnatural. The people were weary of hard times and blatant official stupidity. Trying to relive the past came to seem like a sign of approaching death and degeneration. Society was sick of trite mottoes, ideology, and the tiresome language of power. It hungered for a new leader; a new language of power; and, of course, new causes.

Of course, not all my dreams were fulfilled. The hard-liners who organized the attempted overthrow in 1991 interrupted the reformation of the USSR and hindered the reformation of the Communist Party into a social-democratic party. But they could not abrogate the most important thing. The destruction of the totalitarian system had become an irreversible process.

Ikeda: In trying to define the terms by which to measure our lives, you raise a question as old as humanity. Should life be evaluated in terms of money, property, power, or fame? What you say is correct. Most important of all is the respect of children and of those close to us. Fathers and mothers who lose the confidence of their children, who cannot, in your terms, see themselves through their children's eyes, are unhappy indeed. Children detect falsehood in parents' behavior faster even than close friends. The American scientist and pacifist Linus Pauling told me that the desire to keep his wife's respect inspired him to speak out against the anticommunist hearings at the height of McCarthyism and to do his utmost for peace.

Your remarks help me understand the motives behind Perestroika better. As I have always thought, they were imbued with a high moral character that inspired you to reject the monstrosity and absurdity of the system you inherited. Your most valorous undertaking was to make the USSR and the Communist Party accord with your own conceptions of the reasonable and just.

Your conscience is your sole judge. You can go shamelessly and fearlessly through life with head held high. In this, you are unlike many other politicians. You were able to give Russia democracy and freedom because your actions were founded on firm moral convictions.

Gorbachev: Yes, my initial moral position was one factor in making my choice of freedom irreversible. Even in childhood, though I did not understand its deep causes, I sensed the injustice of the tragedy of the second half of the 1930s. Serious reflection on history began during my years of study at Moscow University, especially in my period of political and social activity.

I experienced no miraculous transformations. Anyone with a normal soul and a minimum of moral feeling could see that the political powers despised the people and paid little attention to their questionings or to their dignity. Having grown up in a rural setting, I saw the Stalinist regime treating peasants like serfs. It is not surprising that rural people were quicker than city-dwellers to doubt the justice of the existing order.

My fellow students at Moscow State considered concepts like collectivization and the kolkhoz system only from a theoretical viewpoint. For me they were realities. From personal experience, I knew how much injustice there was in them both. Real life intruded on the study process, fracturing bookish interpretations of society.

Ikeda: Collectivization resulted in the starvation of millions. According to one noted Russian writer, nothing like it had ever been done before— not by the tsars, not by the Mongols, and not by the invading Nazis.

Gorbachev: Nonetheless, some people today still try to justify this tragedy. During my student years, I witnessed an unbridled campaign to expose what was called "stateless cosmopolitanism" and "servility to the West". This campaign provided occasion for unrestrained anti-Semitic attacks in which Jews were accused of treachery. Vile and unjust, the attacks evoked protest.

First, as a member of the Komsomol youth organization and then as a party worker, I did whatever I could, within the framework of the system, to make life better for people. Reaching the conclusion that reforms were necessary required a great deal of learning, thinking, and understanding. I was not the only one who had to think and learn. Of course, dissidents and democratically inclined intellectuals gave much thought to such matters during the 1960s. But I am thinking not of them, but of members of the party and government nomenklatura. Because of their involvement, it can be said that the reform initiative grew up within the party itself. Several times it overflowed in the form of reform decisions and finally was regenerated as Perestroika.

Society needed cardinal reforms. But the prevailing system undermined programs of renovation. In the course of our reforms, however, we went further than anything undertaken previously: we pioneered a path out of totalitarianism and to freedom and democracy. Condemning spiritual and political oppression, we broke once and for all with Stalinism. But I never thought it permissible to adopt a nihilistic attitude toward the past. Our fathers and grandfathers did not live in vain. Inspired by communistic ideas, they achieved much that was great.

Ikeda: A few years ago Japanese television showed a series of documentaries called "Socialism in the Twentieth Century". In one of them, an old woman who had survived man-made famine in the Ukraine during the 1930s said, as she dried her eyes: "People were so hungry that they stole other people's children and ate them."

The horrors of that famine were apocalyptic. In his book *Everything Flows*, Vladimir Grossman (1905–64) describes the nightmare in all its drama:

Not since the Russian government came into being has such an order been given. No tsar, no Mongol Tartar, and no German invader ever signed such an order. Do you mean to say that the order meant death by starvation for peasants in the Ukraine, on the Don, and in the Kuban? Even killed little children? Ah, I see. For the Soviet authorities, nothing but the Plan mattered. Fulfill the Plan! Carry out the Plan! Give us our allotments, give us government issue. The government comes first. The people don't count.

Under the tsars, in time of much less severe famines, everything was done to help the hungry. But at the beginning of the 1930s, people died beside local barns packed with so-called state reserves.

Together with the Holocaust, Stalinist collectivization is one of the most terrifying tragedies of the 20th century. It poses many unprecedented questions. How can we explain Stalin's unheard-of, universal cruelty? How could he deliberately destroy tens of millions of the old Russian peasantry and virtually deracinate Ukrainians, Russians, and others?

How does a man who has decided to kill millions feel? What in Stalin arose from his own soul and what from the Marxist ideology he professed? Why in a land that suffered so much from him do some people—even whole parties—still worship Stalin the monster? In drawing conclusions about the 20th century, we do not have the right to forget the hideous crimes the Bolsheviks committed against the peoples of the USSR.

Gorbachev: My generation preserved its faith in the socialist ideal and thought that all the trouble resulted from a perversion of socialism. Perestroika was evoked by an effort to conform reality to the ideal and to get rid of what we called the deformation of socialism. Consequently, we were not dissidents in the exact meaning of the word. We were more revisionists of real socialism and advocates of its renovation.

When I was chosen general secretary of the Central Committee of the Communist Party of the Soviet Union, apparently I had a choice: either to preserve the system we had inherited in its unaltered form or to initiate reforms. Actually, I had no choice: the nation impatiently awaited reform.

Today, not a few people speculate about the motives behind Perestroika and about the aims my confederates and I set in 1985 when we started the democratic transformation of the country. Some say that the Soviet Union's technical lag behind the United States forced Gorbachev toward Perestroika or that there was never anything behind Perestroika but naked state pragmatism and determination to preserve the existing system at any cost. Others try to connect Perestroika with

Gorbachev's supposed innate ambition and desire to be a hero. Both radical democrats and frenzied patriots try to defame Perestroika—some out of lack of conscience, others out of lack of sense.

Ikeda: It is impossible to convince the unknowing what morality is. They cannot be convinced that some politicians are guided by upright feelings, are incapable of oppressing their compatriots, and suffer because in their country dissidence is persecuted and people are imprisoned for their political views. It is more than odd that the people who do not believe in the moral motivation of Perestroika are the very ones who repeatedly extol Russian spirituality on every street corner and insist that spiritual values are supreme for the Russian people. Surely Khrushchev, who dared to criticize the Stalinist repressions, was a Russian? Is it possible that your opponents can deny your right to being a Russian and to defend the unity of politics and morality?

Soka Gakkai and Moscow State University began forming ties in the early 1970s. Since then, my colleagues and I have observed the gradual liberation from Marxist dogma in your country. People grew freer year by year. They became bolder in making contacts with foreigners and spoke louder about the shortcomings of Soviet life.

Represented by writers like Rasputin, Zalygin, and Astaf'ev, your literature freed itself from ideological fetters and appealed to a sense of conscience. It exposed the horrors of collectivization, Stalinist repressions, and famine. It posed the age-old questions of human life. I believe that Solzhenitsyn was surprised to learn that the party powers permitted Rasputin, Astaf'ev, and Belov to write the kind of things for which he was exiled from the USSR.

We observed how people—especially the intellectuals—waited and believed that the ideological dictatorship would end and the time of free thought would come. And indeed, when you came into power, the turning point was reached.

Gorbachev: Short memory is the major failing of critics of Perestroika. They have apparently forgotten what the moral and psychological situation in the country had become by 1985. Everybody—leaders and ordinary citizens alike—physically sensed that things had gone wrong.

A series of general secretaries' funerals started with Brezhnev's death in 1982. The ruling summit was clearly breaking down morally and spiritually. The level of social education and the spiritual and intellectual needs of the broadest echelons of the technical and humanitarian intelligentsia were separated by the most scandalous and absurd contradictions from the Marxist-Leninist dogmas advertised by an immense propaganda machine.

Ikeda: To forget the past is fearsome. Of course, nothing good comes of petty rancor. But if we forget the facts of history, our future will be dim. This is especially pertinent to Japanese history amnesiacs. Before World War II, Japanese invaders caused other peoples immeasurable suffering. Today, some Japanese politicians repudiate all Japanese culpability. No wonder they are sharply criticized.

Gorbachev: I agree that oblivion is fearsome. People who have no memory have no future. Without memory there is no responsibility. Without memory it is impossible to understand and correctly evaluate the times.

Critics of Perestroika—who are legion in the ranks of the liberal intelligentsia—try to cast doubt on the motives prompting me to start reforms. They have simply forgotten what they themselves thought and dreamed about on the eve of the plenary session of the Party Central Committee in March 1985.

At the end of the 20th century, the level of education in the Soviet Union was among the highest in the world. Still people were imprisoned for political reasons, and free thought was suppressed and persecuted. We were forbidden to read the works of such Silver-Age Russian philosophers as Nikolai Berdyaev, Sergei Bulgakov, and Semyon Frank. We were unable to make use of the works of outstanding pre-Revolutionary historians like Klyuchevsky, Solovyov, and Karamzin. Because of their high educational level and moral development, the people could no longer accept the ossified dogma about class and class morality. They were no longer willing to countenance the monopoly of a single ideology.

But another factor—often overlooked—stimulated Perestroika. In the 1970s and the first half of the 1980s, East European socialist nations exerted a far greater influence on the moral and political situation in the USSR than Western nations did. The Prague Spring of 1968, the reforms of Janos Kádár in Hungary, and the events of 1980 in Poland aroused the Soviet intelligentsia.

When I was elected secretary general in 1985, I no longer faced the problem of choosing whether to initiate reforms. In its essence, Perestroika was not a choice for me: it was a direct extension of my personality, my philosophy, and my moral feelings.

Today, the originators of the dirtiest, most cynical attacks on me are the very ones who received freedom at my hands, who gained power over people's minds thanks to the openness policy called Glasnost. Perestroika deprived some people of the power and privileges of command. It pushed them from the saddle of unaccountability. Their hatred of me is explainable. But malicious mudslinging from people to whom I extended the hand of assistance in difficult times, whom I literally helped to their feet, is hard to understand. Such is the enigma of the human spirit.

Ikeda: The people who acquired power thanks to you, and through it amassed enormous fortunes, were not democratic in your way. Morality and compassion are foreign to them. They wanted unbridled power and struggled less with communism and totalitarianism than with anyone who stood in the way of their right to govern. After 1991, they turned away from you because you were—and remain—a living reproach to them. You know things they wish to conceal, perhaps even from themselves.

We cannot expect justice and compassion from people who do not know what justice and compassion are. Nonetheless, we must always be prepared to show compassion. As my mentor Josei Toda used to say, "Compassion is precious, but we have no right to demand it. We can recommend compassionate behavior but cannot complain of its lack. The Buddhist must be compassionate but must not demand compassion from others."

Gorbachev: I have never expected people to answer compassion with compassion. But I did expect the observance of normal human relations, if only from the recipients of my help. The opposite is what I got. It is not necessary to answer compassion with compassion, but why should people answer compassion with malice and hatred? That is the question. Still, even after I had shaken off the neophyte reformer's delusions and had seen the true face of our "democratic intelligentsia", I kept my faith in humanity.

Probably the reactions I encountered were only to be expected of people just emerging from a totalitarian past. Stalinism corrupted executioners and victims alike. Treachery became the sickness of everyone associated with it. They all fell under its influence.

In spite of everything, my original convictions remain unchanged. Trust and belief in humanity are still the major elements of my disposition.

Lev Tolstoy believed that equality permeates all human culture and that there can be no morality, no religion, and no creativity without it. I am profoundly convinced that, in addition to being pragmatically constructive, the sense of organic equality with one's own kind is important to good spiritual health. Nothing is more destructive than the tendency to preach, reprimand, and pontificate. Respect for your partner as an equal evokes the best aspects of his spirit and awakens him to candor and creative impulses.

Everyone has the right of self-assertion and the right to protect his or her interests. The important thing is to listen to what the other party has to say. Human relations are formed on the basis of moral principles. While manifesting individual characteristics each person has the capability of being one part in the whole of civic society. I feel certain that the growth of individual liberty is a necessary condition for the growth of overall liberty.

Ikeda: I agree entirely. As long as it remains a mere abstract slogan, "Equality" can imperceptibly degenerate into blind discrimination and exploitation. But, if we live it—instead of merely proclaiming it—equality can be real.

Shakyamuni advocated equality by strongly opposing the caste system. When a certain Brahmin asked him about his birth, he replied, "I am neither Brahmin nor prince. Nor do I belong to the Vaisya [the third of the four Hindu castes, made up of farmers, merchants, and businessmen] or to any other caste. I wear simple clothes and have no home. I shave my beard and head. My spirit is pure and peaceful. And thus I travel about this world."

Shakyamuni did more than teach equality. He lived according to its principle. The Buddhist Order, or Sangha, is said to have been based on the republican system of government adhered to by certain tribes of Shakyamuni's day. All of its members were equal. Admission to the Sangha was unconditional. Some of Shakyamuni's disciples are recorded as having come from the most despised social classes.

Gorbachev: For this reason, Buddhism is a worldwide and universal, not merely an ethnic, religion. The philosophy of equality is fundamental, but liberalism cannot substitute for all other forms of thought.

Other things are important too. For instance, one of the principal lessons I learned from my struggle as a politician is this: under no circumstances can we allow suspension of our illusions to undermine faith in the reason and conscience of the people from whom we derive our substance. A politician without faith in the creative powers of his people is dead. He himself becomes incapable of all creativity and of achieving anything great.

In essence, my reforming initiatives were motivated most of all by the faith that, once liberated, the Soviet people would manifest creative energy. To those of us undertaking Perestroika, it was clear that communist totalitarianism and Stalinist socialism were founded on fear of the people and lack of faith in their spiritual forces. As we began Perestroika, we first of all strove to overcome the habit of regarding the people as cheap merchandise or a submissive labor force. The first motto we proclaimed for domestic use—as you might say—was "Don't fear your own people". I stood by that principle, even when it was perilous even to discuss such things. Now that the democratic revolution in Russia is a hard fact, my faith in the people has become something sacred.

Am I happy? That is a difficult question to answer. I still regret that I did not manage to bring the ship I piloted into peaceful waters. I was unable to complete the process of reforming the USSR.

But, in the broader view, I was fated to lead one of the most important revolutions of the 20th century. In that sense, I can be called lucky. I knocked on the doors of history, and they opened to me and to all of us. The threat of general nuclear catastrophe no longer hangs over our heads.

Ikeda: You are greatly to be envied. You attained the impossible and accomplished what no other Russian leader has ever dared to do. You fulfilled your people's centuries-old dream. You gave them freedom of political choice. Restoring their historical memory, you presented them with the blessings of contemporary civilization and opened the USSR to the whole world. What they make of their political freedoms and their restored spiritual and cultural values is up to them. Sooner or later the citizens of your country will have—if not the gratitude—at least the self-respect to appreciate the immense merit of your reforms. At your own risk and on your own responsibility you achieved what the Russian and Soviet intelligentsia had dreamed about.

It seems to me that the Russians cannot evaluate themselves or their sense of history as they deserve without an objective and honest evaluation of Perestroika. If it is forgotten, much of 20th-century Russian history will be incomprehensible.

While welcoming the removal of the threat of general nuclear catastrophe, the West tends to associate Perestroika with the so-called defeat of the USSR in the Cold War. Itself redolent of Cold-War attitudes, this approach ignores the moral and spiritual courage the Soviet people displayed in freeing themselves, without aid or bloodshed, from the remnants of their Stalinist heritage. Ultimately, undervaluing Perestroika leads to undervaluing the very possibility of progress and the potentiality of contemporary civilization.

Gorbachev: I consider my own mission unfinished. Having chosen the path of reform and freedom, I shall stand up for it as long as I live. The spiritual and political capital I have amassed must be used in the name of the freedom of my country and the security of human civilization. I consider myself sufficiently strong to continue my work.

In the summer of 1986, a few months after the twenty-seventh congress of the Party, I put the question of democracy point-blank to the Politburo. The core of this question is faith in the people. I insisted then that the most important sphere of Perestroika is democratization. I said there was no need to fear democracy—questions, problems, and discussions—at any level, from the Politburo to the smallest collectives and the family circle.

Ikeda: I am glad to hear this from you. When I asked Arnold J. Toynbee what his motto was, he replied with the Latin verb *Laboremus*— Let us work. Such a positive approach to life represents what in Buddhism is called the attitude of the "true cause". Happiness and an awareness of it are found in the ceaseless accumulation of such causes in the instant-by-instant process of self-perfection. This is the quintes-sential Buddhist way of life. The person who is always guided by devotion to unending progress and limitless hope is perennially a victor.

Reform or Revolution from Below

Ikeda: On your initiative, Perestroika was reform from above. But by its very nature democratization must be carried out at the same time from below, taking advantage of the dispositions of broad popular strata. I can imagine therefore the immense difficulties the dilemma of manag-ing democratic reforms must have caused you.

Obviously, if you had not restrained pressure from below—had not controlled the energy of the masses—mere political overthrow would have been succeeded by chaos instead of freedom. At the same time, restraining popular energy could have evoked distrust of Perestroika and its leaders and conflict between those who revolutionized from above and those who revolutionized from below.

As history shows, traditional Russian political awareness seems to require an authoritarian approach. Sometimes Russian reforms have exceeded popular willingness to accept them. Occasionally, they imposed unfamiliar norms. The Russian philosopher Chaadaev was probably correct in saying that for Peter the First, Russia was only a sheet of white paper on which to scrawl the words "Europe" and "the West". Chaadaev added: "We belong to Europe and the West. Make no mistake, no matter how great the genius of the man [Peter I] and no matter how unusual the energy of his will, what he did was possible only among nations whose traditions are powerless to create a future and whose recollections a bold legislator can erase with impunity."

Energetic leadership propagating knowledge in ignorance and setting people on the right path inevitably earns a good reputation for enlightenment or a bad one for authoritarianism. Peter I—the Tsar Enlightener—embodied this dilemma.

Some Japanese intellectuals claimed that your methods of conducting Perestroika were reminiscent of the reforms of Peter I. Of course, this is only a superficial comparison. We must not equate the two simply because both proceeded from above. Although, as general secretary of the Communist Party, you had unbounded power, you deliberately subjected your reforms to the authority of law. This was the genius of your method. It was done for the sake of evolving the process of democratization. Ironically, as it gathered impetus, this process began undermining the foundation of your power.

All of this shows how rocky the road to democratization is in Russia, where people are disturbed by unstable conditions and the danger of further destruction. Some of them dream of returning to the strong-arm methods of Peter I (at his best) if only to avoid chaos. Still, I want to believe that, in spite of difficulties and reversals, the course of Perestroika will not be reversed.

How has your experience with Perestroika affected your outlook on democratic government? Do you think it possible to compare Perestroika with the reforms of Peter I? What in your reforms resulted from the expectations and aspirations of the people?

Gorbachev: The reforms of Peter I were neither a motivation nor a model for my reforms, at any rate in a direct form. That said, however, I must remark that the image of Peter the Reformer is always with us Russians. We react to him in two ways. We respect him for—as we learned as children—opening a window on the West and cultivating the spirit of education. But we also remember what our famous historian Klyuchevsky had to say about him: "Peter acted on the force of power, not the mind, and counted not on the people's moral motives, but on their instincts. Running the government from camp wagons and post stations, he thought only about business, not about people. Confident in the strength of his authority, he insufficiently considered the passive power of the masses." Most important of all, Klyuchevsky pointed out: "In his reforming dashing about, Peter never stopped to think about the limitations of human strength."

Perestroika arose in a completely different context in Russian history. Of course, some people, especially members of the intelligentsia, were impatient to pull the Iron Curtain down. In that sense, we too faced the problem of opening a window on Europe—or more exactly, on the world.

Strongest of all, however, was our desire to settle accounts with the Stalinist heritage in both politics and ways of thinking. We wanted to settle with the pernicious habit of deciding for the people. The desire to restore the rule of law and justice and to find out the truth about our history motivated us. This spirit and these hopes differ entirely from those of the beginning of the 18th century.

In the broad view, our upward drive took the form of striving to protect the individual and his right to personal happiness, initiative, and his own opinions.

Ikeda: I am not overlooking the barbarous methods and cruel violence of Peter's reforms. As you have pointed out, reforms and enlightenment imposed from above have many aspects, all of which must be considered. Nonetheless, a public opinion poll conducted not too long ago showed that, among the Russians, Peter I is the most popular figure in history. Marshal Zhukov came in a close second. If memory serves, Lenin came in tenth. Peter's popularity gave me an idea of the magnitude of your achievement in rejecting the cult of violence and everything connected with it in Russian history and of the enormous difficulties you encountered.

We thought the Soviet people were largely unprepared for free, democratic elections. We assumed that, since they could not know how to use it, they were incapable of accepting the freedom offered them.

They were seeking what Dostoyevsky called "somebody to bow to", when you confronted them with the dilemma of political choice. A similar situation obtained—and may persist today—in postwar Japan, where the seeds of the parliamentary system were sown in unprepared ground. That is why the Liberal-Democratic Party governed us for more than 30 years.

Gorbachev: That was precisely the source of the difficulties I sometimes ran into in the course of Perestroika. As you say, rejecting the past presupposed the rejection of the cult of violence and everything connected with it in Russian history. The people were tired of the cult of sacrifice, which, by the way, had already become firmly established in the time of Peter I. Only dogmatists, aggressive patriots and—by their nature—neo-Stalinists insisted that Russia must remain a mobilized structure and employ mobilization as a means of making the people work. Such people were and remain irreconcilable enemies of Perestroika, which emphasizes initiative, free will, and free choice above all.

Ikeda: You were absolutely correct to say that the people were tired of the ideology of sacrifice. Still, for better or worse, the endurance and patience of the Russian people are truly astonishing. They not only patiently endured the impudent flouting of human rights by the Stalinist regime for over half a century, but also in many cases voluntarily sacrificed themselves like martyrs. In the industrialization period, they performed wonders of heroic labor. Naked and barefoot in the cold and mud, they built mills, factories, and new towns, asking nothing in return.

Then, during privatization in the 1990s—to the distress of people of conscience all over the world—all the valuable things created by generations of Soviet citizens were cynically doled out to a group of so-called oligarchs. The Russians' long-suffering nature has a religious element. No other people could bear what your people have endured and still endure.

Against this background, the messianism of the Russian Orthodox Church is understandable. Universally, a sense of mission stimulates future-oriented movement, even in the face of the gravest difficulties. But there is a limit to everything. Though capable of noble self-sacrifice, human beings harbor shameless animal instincts, causing them callously to sacrifice others to their own greed.

As early as the 1930s, the philosopher Nikolai Berdyaev identified the cult of the ideology of sacrifice as the weak point in communism: "The Soviet philosophy is a philosophy of social Titanism. The Titan is not the individual, but the social collective. It is omnipotent. It has no need even of the laws of nature, the baseness of which belongs to bourgeois science and philosophy." You wanted to liberate the individual from this Titanism in the name of the human factor, which played a paramount role in Perestroika.

Gorbachev: Much in current conditions in Russia displeases me. Still, I am glad that the philosophy of sacrifice has been exhausted. I do not entirely agree with Berdyaev. The triumph of self-interest—although it bloomed luxuriantly in Russia—is not the only reason why enthusiasm dried up.

The naked fervor that had devoured human lives finally discredited itself. No one wants to die for the sake of a chimera. Note well that often great enthusiasm is accompanied by the absence of thought. In *Cursed*

Days the great Russian writer Ivan A. Bunin discerned indifference behind patriotic Russian upsurges. He said that this indifference arises from the "terribly innate [Russian] carelessness, frivolity, and habitual desire to be flippant in the most serious of moments". In general, I agree that we require thought and responsibility more than messianism and sacrifice.

Ikeda: To bring the human factor of Perestroika into play in the creation of a really democratic society, it was necessary to overcome self-estrangement from reality. We Japanese, who are prone to collectivism, must realize that what happened in Russia could conceivably happen in Japan too. Russian events are good examples from which we may draw useful lessons. There is no straight road from communist Titanism directly to the free, spiritually rich individual. The fall of collectivism itself does not lead automatically to the emergence of the whole, responsible, individual personality. Patently, removal of Soviet bans and restrictions led to willfulness and caprice among socially isolated fringes. Liberalism tainted with mercenary cynicism is harmful.

Gorbachev: Today in Russia many people argue over the roots and outlooks of liberalism in our country. Not long ago, the Gorbachev Foundation devoted a meeting of a traditional political-science seminar to that theme. Some insisted that, by its nature, Russian culture is foreign to liberalism and Russians totally lack instincts for property and freedom. Others insisted that ideals of liberalism are consonant with both Russian culture and Russian history. To my way of thinking, such argument makes no sense. On the eve of Perestroika, the public mood was undoubtedly shifting in the direction of liberalism and liberation from bondage. I mention this in response to your question about the degree to which Russians are predisposed to civil initiatives.

Undeniably, at the end of the 1970s and the beginning of the 1980s, a spontaneous, sometimes conscious movement arose against the system of bans that had fettered freedom and initiative. Scholars discussed liberalization of the market and market–money relations, development of cooperation, and more flexible forms of union between private and social interests. From the middle of the 1960s, the role and place of market–money relations under socialism were constantly discussed. All of these were liberal moods leading ultimately to the rehabilitation of the market and of private initiative.

The intelligentsia waged war in the name of creative liberty and freedom of discussion. Please remember that, in the political report made to the twenty-seventh congress of the Communist Party of the Soviet Union, solutions to pressing problems are tied to development of initiative and strengthening of economic stimuli. To be faithful to historical truth, we must admit that the demand for change ripened first in society and was, in that sense, from below.

Ikeda: Your own personal experience suggests that seeds of freedom were already being sown at the twilight of the Stalin epoch. In 1945, after the end of World War II, Stalin was unable to restore the old fear and repression. After the Khrushchev thaw, the axis of the Stalinist system was broken. Kosygin tried to restore the health of the socialist economy by initiating economic reforms and introducing market mechanisms. (I met him twice and found him pleasant to talk with and different from other party leaders.) But his reforms failed and, 20 years later, more fundamental measures had become urgently needed.

Gorbachev: We must take into account circumstances connected with the specific nature of reforms in the communist kingdom that the Soviet Union really was. Only reforms compatible with official ideology were conceivable. No one—not even the secretary-general of the Central Committee of the Communist Party of the Soviet Union—had the right to contradict the principles of Marxism-Leninism. Inevitably, anyone who tried to do so would be accused of deviation and of betraying the interests of the party and the laboring classes.

There could be no appeal to any other historical authority, not even Peter I. Lenin and only Lenin was above suspicion. Our generation really believed—and probably not without grounds—that if Lenin had remained alive and if the New Economic Policy (NEP) he started had continued, forced collectivization and Stalinist terror and repression would never have taken place. We regarded everything that happened in the Soviet Union after 1929 as a deviation from the evolutionary building of socialism that Lenin created in those final works that came to be called his political testament.

When I became general secretary, we were able to cite Lenin's own ideas against dogmatism and stagnation, against communist romanticism, and, of course, in favor of democracy. Doing so was the only way to make a breakthrough in the direction of good sense. And, indeed, this was the course many scholars and the new leadership followed in promoting reform. We insisted that, as a scholar and politician, Lenin gave preeminence to reality, not a-priori schemes. We quoted him as saying: "We must start with what is... from the absolutely established."

Even when exceeding the framework of established socialist conceptions we cited Lenin, who urged a change in our whole view of socialism. Perestroika, in other words, began under the banner of later Lenin.

Ikeda: I consider slow, gradual reforms and small breaks within the framework of an established system more beneficial than revolution, in which the break with the past is unexpected and impulsive. People who, at their own risk, began reforms within the existing economic ideology merit as much respect as heroes of the barricades and insurgents heedlessly defying all obstacles. You and your comrades-in-arms in the Soviet Union played just as revolutionary a role as, for instance, Solidarity in Poland. This no doubt accounts for the particular nature of democratic reforms in Russia. I agree that Lenin was pragmatic and that, in some respects, his NEP amounts to a revision of Marxism. I doubt, however, that even if he had remained alive and persevered with the NEP he would have assumed the social-democratic position you assumed. He remained a prisoner to ideological intolerance. For instance, as is generally admitted, even during the NEP period of economic indulgences, Lenin repressed the clergy.

The hero in Anatoly Rybakov's widely discussed novel *Children of the Arbat* thinks: "What is morality? Lenin said morality is whatever is in the interests of the proletariat. But the proletariat is made up of people, and proletarian morality is human morality. Abandoning children in the snow is inhuman, consequently immoral. And it's immoral to save your own life at the cost of somebody else's."

In a country ruled by an official ideology, citing Lenin was the only way to break through the blank ideological wall and have the human being recognized as the prime value. And, as Buddhism teaches, we must select, revive and make use of whatever good things we find in any philosophy or ideology.

Gorbachev: Your comments on my stance on Lenin are correct. But it is important to remember certain things. First, I remain faithful to the socialist idea. Second, Lenin is an integral part of Russian history, and we must take him seriously. He played an enormous role in the history of all humanity.

The interesting thing about Lenin for me is the connection he draws between communism and intellectual progress and his insistence that communism must enrich itself by calling on all human knowledge. In my youth, as a worker in the communist youth organization Komsomol, I propagandized Leninist ideas. I will remain true to them to the end. Still, I agree with you that his interpretation of morality is uncertain and mistaken. This is precisely why we began our ideological revolution with a rejection of the class interpretation of morality.

Politically speaking, ours was a revolution from above. Essentially, at the time and under those circumstances any other kind of reform was impossible. Even if they had occurred, reforms from below would only have meant civil war. Indeed, if we had failed to initiate democratic reforms, as dissatisfaction mounted, such a thing might have happened. The option of gradual democratic reforms from below did not exist. We had to choose between either a revolution from above, ensuring gradual transformation, or revolution from below, accompanied as it always is by blood and destruction.

We must also remember that the Soviet Union totally lacked a powerful, legal, Western-style, opposition movement. There are many reasons for this. The Soviet totalitarian system was far harsher and more merciless than systems in, for instance, Eastern European countries such as Hungary and, especially, Poland. Immediately after Soviet troops were sent into Czechoslovakia in 1968, dissidents in the USSR suffered cruel persecutions. Of course, the Soviet dissident movement—notably the human-rights activities of Andrei Dmitriyevich Sakharov—had enormous moral significance. But they lacked political strength and a political base.

In spite of rising social dissatisfaction, especially among the intelligentsia, there was no mass protest movement to political transformation. This lack complicated the situation for several reasons. The habit of a significant part of the population to put up with things, the traditional Russian long-suffering attitude, and the hope that things would work themselves out—deeply rooted in ancient Russian tradition, these traits were deformed and intensified during the decades of the merciless Stalinist regime and remained essentially unshaken in the post-Stalin period.

In the countries of Eastern Europe—again especially in Poland—relying on the mighty support of the consistently independent Catholic Church, the opposition intelligentsia nudged the ruling communist party to renovate socialism. In this case, the opposition emerged as the subject and initiator of democratic transformation.

Everything was different with us. On the strength of the prevailing social mood and expectations of change, reformers within the Central Committee created an opposition by permitting freedom of speech and the press. Almost all forces operating on the political scene—reformers, social-communists working against Perestroika, and radical democrats—emerged from the party nomenklatura.

This indicates a number of things. First, it shows that, in the Soviet Union, reforms could start only at the top, with the initiative of the party leadership. Second, it indicates that, in the early stage, reforms could be directed only at perfecting the existing system and could proceed only within the framework of that system. Third, it meant that only evolutionary transformation which eroded the foundations of total-itarianism from within had any hope of success.

Ikeda: Under your leadership and in good faith the Communist Party initiated democratic reforms. Not surprisingly, therefore, no so-called trial of the party ever took place. It might have been just to bring to court Lenin, Trotsky, and Stalin, the three leaders who inundated the land with blood. But it would have been amoral to try you, the leader of the party that had the good will to give the people their freedom. Who would have been the judges? Your opposing such a false judgment of the Communist Party was good. We must condemn repression and crimes against humanity. But it is impossible to condemn a country's history. Still, for us, the motives of your reforms remain a riddle.

Gorbachev: As I have said, we did not make the choice in favor of change lightly. Children of the times, we were all in the power of ideo-logical dogmas and stereotyped ways of thinking imbibed from infancy. Deliverance from them took place in complicated, diverse, and unsyn-chronized ways. Some of us finished the course quickly. Some stopped halfway. Still others took a few steps forward then, frightened by possible responsibility and—most of all—frightened by possible consequences, regressed.

Even after we started reforms—the policy of Glasnost and a new Russian revolution from above—how could we foresee the details of all subsequent steps, all possible consequences of the democratic transfor-mation? Remember the West had no faith at all in the possibility of democratic changes in Russia. For a long time, many Westerners—for instance, Kremlinologists in the United States—refused to take us seri-ously.

The transformation of communism into democracy was unprece-dented. Mistakes were inevitable. I do not, however, acquit myself of moral responsibility for all the negative processes brought to life. No prognosis or strategic plan is complete. All bear the impress of human biases and the illusions of their time.

Glasnost at the Crossroads

Ikeda: Perestroika once again demonstrated the paramount impor-tance of the words: "In the beginning was the Word." Your experiment with openness, or Glasnost, has unique global historical significance. But, in Japan, it is insufficiently understood from the philosophical and historical viewpoints. The Russian experience suggests that merely allowing human beings to express their thoughts and feelings freely is enough to change a whole nation.

As long as it remains unexpressed, the thought embodies only the possibility of change. As soon as it is voiced, however, it explodes into action. Truth uttered aloud is critical in changing public awareness and the political system itself. The policy of Glasnost destroyed the Soviet system by making the truth about it accessible. In two years, your decision to do away with censorship and lift the ban on Solzhenitsyn and other writers and thinkers completely altered the Soviet spiritual climate, in the process winning over doubters in the West.

Gorbachev: I have related the motives and reasons urging us to begin with Glasnost: that is, with lifting bans on the truth. Ardent Soviet ideologists had two groups of opponents: the anticommunists and the philosophers and historians striving to unite socialism and humanism and give preeminence to the ideal of the harmoniously developed individual. During the 1970s, certain ideological processes censured attempts by creative Marxists to conform state ideology to the demands of the epoch. Anyone who still believed in Marxism and socialism but attempted to revitalize the socialist ideal was condemned. The propaganda machine and the ideological system tried to convince the people that conclusions reached in earlier times in a different historical context remained stable.

Attempts to voice doubt on any postulate, as on the ideological system itself, met with merciless punishment. Scientists found themselves out of work and, if they were party members, without their party cards. People who openly disputed such developments fell under vigilant KGB surveillance.

But already, by the beginning of the 1980s, ideological bans no longer worked. Glasnost was on the way. To be sure, it started as a system of political education within the Central Committee. Closed party hearings received more or less correct information about the real situation of the Soviet economy, the reasons for crises in socialist countries, and so on. The general public was able to garner the facts from overseas radio. Thus, by the beginning of Perestroika, bans on information both failed to have the desired ideological effects and provoked wide popular dissatisfaction, most notably among the intelligentsia.

When we set out on the road to Perestroika, the issue of freedom of information came first and foremost. The leadership of the reform wing of the Communist Party had to take the initiative in liberating society from censorship and bans.

Ikeda: Not unexpectedly, the romance of Glasnost faded quickly. In the first years of Perestroika, the openly proclaimed truth about collectivization and repression rocked the nation. Later, however, all interest in Soviet history and the crimes of the Bolsheviks evaporated, as did moral indignation against violence and evil. Moral feelings seem to have been dulled. The people were content to learn the whole truth. The morality that played a decisive role in the collapse of the communist system seems to have lost its vigor.

We who live in a capitalist society find this understandable. The problem of surviving takes precedence over everything else. Truth beckons and attracts as long as it is forbidden fruit. People forget about it when it becomes as accessible as air. Nonetheless, I am disturbed by the possibility that such forgetfulness conceals apathy and cynicism. History offers many examples of liberals and conservatives alike who, having become apathetic and cynical about truth, have been manipulated by false prophets and charlatans.

We must be sensitive to the language of truth. Among contemporary politicians, Václav Havel, president of the Czech Republic and an outstanding dramatist, demonstrates the most refined sensitivity to it. He says that, unlike honest words that fill society with the spirit of freedom, some words are hypnotic and false. He warns against words that arouse fanaticism. Such frenzied and deceiving words, he says, are dangerous and lead even to death. When he asks what the words of Christ were like, he poses the question: Were they the beginning of salvation, the mightiest impulse to cultural creation in the history of the world? Or were they the Crusades, heretic trials, or the uprooting of indigenous cultures by the colonizers of America and the spiritual progeny of expansion? We are asked to think about words that reflect the contradictions of the white race.

To keep from drowning in the contemporary torrent of information, we must remember that verbal truth amounts to a philosophical interpretation of the fundamental problems of life and death. Glasnost and its survival depend on verbal honesty and sincerity.

Gorbachev: Today, lots of people argue that indulgence of nonconformism and the Glasnost policy tore the Soviet Union apart. According to them, the people were unready for freedom of expression. I disagree. Such critics pine for the old ways or support the present regime—they, by the way, are not notably well disposed towards Glasnost. We must remember too that, at the beginning of Perestroika, the Soviet people were among the best educated in the world. It was simply impossible to preserve and support a deepening level of education in an information vacuum.

You and President Havel are correct in saying that freedom of expression always contains danger. The freedom of evil always accompanies the freedom of good. Freedom of speech can be used to evoke the good and the reasonable or to evoke violence. But does this mean that the Russian people had no right at all to the truth? Does it mean that they will never be adults and will never be able to put information and knowledge to use for their own advantage?

Ikeda: I wholeheartedly support your unshakeable conviction in the usefulness of Glasnost to Russian society. Steve Cohen, an American specialist in Soviet affairs at Princeton University, accurately described the essence of the first stage of Perestroika when he said that you began with faith in the power of the word. Without doubt, Glasnost was the core of Perestroika. But it is not all. We must orient it correctly. To do so, we must be able to discriminate between good, sincere words and words that are false and malicious.

Gorbachev: Because of their national character and political traditions, Russians interpret the freedom they received in their own distinctive way. A significant segment of society equates freedom with license. For example, at one time, it was dangerous to appear drunk on the street. The police picked up drunks and sent them to detoxification centers. They then dispatched reports to the drunks' workplaces. Today, many people drink on the streets. Young people behave any way they like and equate dissipation and dissolution with democracy. Some youth-oriented newspapers defend this so-called democracy. Identifying democracy with anti-culture disturbs me more than anything else.

In the mass, Russians do not welcome liberty as the freedom to choose or as a sense of responsibility for one's life and the well being of one's intimates. In this, no specific individuals are culpable. Our reluctance to accept responsibility is a misfortune arising from insufficient experience with democracy and the undeveloped structure of our civil society. Traditional Russian authoritarianism engendered the ideology of materialism and dependence. I turn again to Ivan Bunin who, in analyzing the reasons why the February Revolution failed, was forced to admit that serfdom was entirely to blame. In *Cursed Days* [*Okayannye dni*] he wrote:

> The *muzhiks* said they had only a vague idea of the new system. In all their lives, they'd seen nothing but their own backyards. Nothing else, including their government, interested them. How can there be government by the people if the people know nothing about government and have no feeling for it or for the Russian land outside their own little plots?

It goes without saying, the period of state socialism and the command-administration did very little to accustom the Russian population to participation in state management. This is why, today, people mistake license for freedom, just as they did after the bourgeois revolution of 1917

Unfortunately, no one is attempting a serious, global, philosophical study of the consequences of collapse and transition from total prohibition to total permissiveness. This is a pity because, in my view, the lessons we are learning about the transition to democracy have universal significance. There is much here to think about.

To be honest, I was sincerely surprised when, in a newspaper account of a speech to the House of Scientists in the academic settlement in Novosibirsk, Aleksandr Solzhenitsyn criticized Glasnost for provoking an "outburst of nationalism and the freedom to carry weapons and commit crime". Perhaps the newspaper distorted his real meaning. After all, as a great Russian thinker, he must understand that Glasnost was precisely a reply to his own summons to live without lies.

Living without lies means telling the whole truth about our tragic 20th-century history, relating everything that happened to us at all times—during the Revolution, collectivization, and the Stalinist repressions. Living without lies means talking about the state of our economy and about our problems. Living without lies means opening closed libraries and permitting people to read things formerly forbidden, to read political thinkers who emigrated, and all those philosophers and writers who rejected the Revolution.

I cannot believe that Solzhenitsyn fails to understand Glasnost, which first of all meant freedom of expression for Solzhenitsyn himself. Precisely because of freedom of speech and the Glasnost policy, *The Gulag Archipelago* was first printed—in millions of copies—in Russian. Thanks to freedom of speech, many magazines began publishing his *Red Wheel* series. I cannot see what this has to do with growth in crime.

The Glasnost policy is identical with faith in our people. Whoever objects to it has no faith in their spiritual powers.

Ikeda: I cannot imagine what Solzhenitsyn meant by his criticism. Such a great writer must understand that Glasnost has both positive and negative consequences. It conveys the right to speak out and to propagandize ideas. But false prophets have always been ready to put freedom to evil uses. As he must know, criminality is worse in democratic than in totalitarian countries and that contemporary democracies pay a high price for individual liberty and the freedom of choice. He must also know the dramatic contradictions of freedom. He must realize that the transition from totalitarianism to democracy—a transition he called for—is fraught with many unexpected and negative consequences.

Perhaps he was moved by the kind of jealousy great people sometimes entertain for each other, characteristically in European culture. Einstein and the French philosopher Henri Bergson did not get on well. As you know, under the influence of Einstein's theory of relativity, Bergson worked out his own theory of time. Einstein's new discovery in physics enabled Bergson to deepen his philosophical views. On several occasions he sent Einstein words of gratitude and support. But Einstein rebuffed his amicable demonstrations. Had these two great personages understood each other, it would have been enormously fruitful for 20th-century science. But it was not to be.

Great people are frequently intensely private. But I think you can overcome misunderstandings in your relations with Solzhenitsyn. I should not like to see enmity between two such mighty contributors to the liberation of Russia.

Gorbachev: You have almost guessed my intentions. I too think it would be unfitting for Mr Solzhenitsyn and me to engage in crossfire and expose our relationship in the press. Instead, we should meet and explain ourselves to each other honestly. We have plenty to talk about. We had similar aims, but each worked with his own means and employed his own possibilities.

This then is the dilemma: either freedom of speech permitting falsehood and demagogy or censorship repressing creative and spiritual development. The problem is not exclusively Russian. Possibly, however, given the specific character of our history, it assumes a distinctive nature in Russia. The danger that false prophets will make use of the freedom of speech exists everywhere. Nonetheless, in spite of all moral and spiritual catastrophes and all religious, class, and national obscurantism, the survival of good sense, conscience, and faith in human spiritual powers constitutes the meaning of civilization. This being the case, why should those of us who removed the ban on truth and justice lack faith in our own people?

Ikeda: I respect the way you remained magnanimous and retained your faith in a people who proved treacherous and ungrateful to you. I understand why A. Tsipko called your view of the world the diametric opposite of Lenin's. Apparently, magnanimity was not one of his traits. As the great Japanese writer Ryunosuke Akutagawa (1892–1927), a contemporary of Lenin, said to him: "You [Lenin] loved the people more than anything and you despised the people more than anything."

Gorbachev: Citing Berdyaev, you called Lenin a typical Russian phenomenon. Actually many factors coalesced in him: the tradition of Russian nihilism in the Nechayev vein, and the customary Russian worship of "German science" and discipline. Lenin the dogmatic, Lenin bowing before Jacobinism and revolutionary terror is alien to me. My spiritual experience and my whole outlook are different. But, as I have already told you, all of us contemporary Russian politicians were brought up on Lenin and in this sense are all Leninists. This is at least true in terms of Lenin's traditional Russian maximalism, his claim to definitive truth, and his intransigence towards opponents. I part company with traditional Bolshevism in my understanding of democracy and the correlation between morality and politics. This refers to the fundamental principle distinguishing my offspring the "New Thinking". I categorically object to the politics of victimization in which the lives and happiness of living people are sacrificed to abstract ideas, no matter whether in the name of communism, as with Lenin, or in the name of the market, as with Yeltsin.

But to return to freedom of speech and censorship, the issue ultimately was not so much the abolition of censorship as the possibility of democratic development in the USSR and later in Russia. To the best of my understanding, the essence of democracy consists not in procedures or even in the right to general elections—with all its significance—but in faith in the ability of the people to realize their own interests and to control their own historical destiny. From the very outset, Glasnost involved primary issues like the question of popular moral and spiritual health.

Ikeda: The individual and the individual alone should be the master of his or her fate. The individual has the right of self-sacrifice, the right to take mortal risks to defend the interests of intimates, clan, or people. But no one has the right to force the individual to part with life in the name of an abstract idea or to serve politicians' selfish interests. Truth is valuable only when the individual arrives at it himself. Glasnost revealed the difficult, complex road to knowledge of the truth. In the final analysis, democratic growth and maturity indicate a people's strength, wisdom, and ability to discern truth.

Maturity of the soul presupposes self-knowledge. It cannot be attained all at once and without mistakes and misunderstandings. Many of the problems of the new Russian way of life are connected with Glasnost, which was what it had to be. At the same time, it was only what it could be after 70 years of gagging the truth. Glasnost corresponded with the very nature of the move towards truth.

Feudal Japan too banned truth at a time when the people were expected to be obedient and ignorant of the state of affairs. It was as hard for the Japanese people to emerge from those circumstances as it was for the Russians to arrive at truth. Glasnost was an essential—if insufficient—condition in helping the people govern their own destiny.

Gorbachev: Increased volume of information does not automatically stimulate the development of intellectual activity or the ability to think independently. Unfortunately, the modern mass media can manipulatively instill in the human consciousness ideas and thoughts contrary to our own interests. The tendency for such manipulation is especially great in Russia, where people are accustomed to believing everything they hear on the television. When, as is the case with us, independent thought is underdeveloped, the media controllers have the power. This situation can nullify the very principle of free elections.

Distinguishing lies from truth takes experience. Fortunately, as I have learned from associations during my trips around the country, people are sobering up fast. Interestingly, in the Russian provinces, they pay more attention to local than to central television broadcasts. They put their trust in things that are immediately verifiable and related to their own experiences. I have every reason to believe that our people are wise enough to overcome traditional gullibility and starry-eyed idealism.

When the fate of the Soviet Union was being decided, the tragic consequences of allowing the union to split up and of granting sovereignty to the Russian Federation were poorly understood. People failed to see that their own power was on trial and that, essentially, the Belovezh Agreement was a national catastrophe. I appealed to the parliaments of the former Soviet republics to demonstrate prudence and refrain from destroying something that had taken ages to create. But I went unheeded; and, after a few years, the so-called heroes of Belovezh found themselves in moral isolation.

In beginning and expanding freedom of speech our first thoughts were of our successors in state management. We never equated freedom of speech with totally unrestrained license. As we conceived it, Glasnost ought to have led to diametrically opposite results. We restored the right to knowledge of historical truth in the hope of cultivating a sense of historical responsibility and of continuity with our forefathers' way of life.

Ikeda: His whole life long, Nichiren Daishonin, the founder of our faith, defended freedom of expression. Frequently subjected to persecution and oppression, he endured peril and misery. Still, never yielding to pressure from the authorities and never renouncing his convictions, he vindicated his religion through the power of the word. For his followers, his life confirms the surprising power the word can exert when reinforced by faith and conviction. Undaunted by mortal danger, Nichiren Daishonin affirmed:

> Whether tempted by good or threatened by evil, if one casts aside the Lotus Sutra, one destines oneself for hell. Here I will make a great vow. Though I might be offered the rulership of Japan if I would only abandon the Lotus Sutra, accept the teachings of the Meditation Sutra, and look forward to rebirth in the Pure Land, though I might be told that my father and mother will have their heads cut off if I do not recite the Nembutsu—whatever obstacles I might encounter, so long as persons of wisdom do not prove my teachings to be false, I will never yield! (*The Writings of Nichiren Daishonin*, hereafter *WND* [Tokyo: Soka Gakkai, 1999], p. 280)

Firm in his faith, Nichiren Daishonin began spreading his teachings among the people, attempting to arouse in every person a sense of responsibility and an awareness of his or her self as part of history.

During World War II, in collusion with state Shinto, political authorities subjected Soka Gakkai to cruel pressure. But, true to the teachings of Nichiren Daishonin, our first president Tsunesaburo Makiguchi and our second president Josei Toda never deviated from their chosen path. They demonstrated how, as you say, freedom of speech and religious faith are founded on trust in humanity.

Gorbachev: Though ourselves wary of unrestrained freedom of expression, we knew the people had to be told what they had waited decades to hear. When all is said and done, sooner or later, somebody had to admit that, even when committed in the name of a great idea, a crime is still a crime. The noblest goal cannot justify the suffering of the innocent; progress achieved at the expense of our right to happiness is useless.

Sources of the New Thought

Ikeda: On December 25, 1991, in your farewell television address, without concealing your sadness at the collapse of the USSR, you reminded the citizens of your country of the achievements of Perestroika. Among the most important, you cited the ending of the Cold War and the relaxation of international tension. And indeed, your decision to reject class values in the name of the values of all humanity changed the whole world. Your international politics was founded on the idea that nuclear disaster would render meaningless even the triumph of the international Communist movement. From the very outset, you connected what you called the New Thinking with humanity-wide values. The old world died when this connection was made. In an oft-quoted remark, Einstein said the splitting of the atom changed everything except mankind's way of thinking. Your New Thinking would have dispelled his gloom on this score.

Gorbachev: As an idea, the New Thinking has a long history (Einstein, Russell, and Sakharov). Our service—and it was hard to perform—was to take up the idea and apply it in realistic external policies. Our job was thus to ensure the victory of good sense.

The ideas of a political philosophy were first formulated between December 1984 and April 1985. They developed further between 1986 and 1989 during practical realization of new approaches to contemporary international relations. During this time, we continued to proclaim our devotion to Lenin's ideas of peaceful coexistence between governments belonging to different social systems. Nonetheless, even in the initial stage of Perestroika, we insisted that peaceful coexistence means different things at different stages of cooperation between socialism and capitalism.

For Lenin, peaceful coexistence meant a tactic of truce to gain time for the new system to get on its feet. He was convinced that capitalism would exhaust itself and explode from within. Behind the Leninist formula was the notion of global uniformity and the conviction that, sooner or later, all peoples would be subject to the communist system and that the Marxist variant of social development is the only one. In working out new approaches to international relations, we started with an entirely different philosophical world. Development of human civilization urged us to recognize a great diversity of systems.

Ikeda: The emergence of nuclear arms means that competition among governments can lead to the destruction of humanity. To prevent this, we must transcend the narrow framework of government interests and adopt a world philosophy embracing the interests of all humankind. This is precisely why your proclaiming humanity-wide values from the political arena gave me a sense of profound satisfaction.

Unfortunately, however, the threat of nuclear catastrophe has not gone away. Indeed, it has been compounded by the threat of ecological disaster. Everything depends on our ability to give absolute pride of place to values of all humanity and, primarily, to life itself. We are in great need of Albert Schweitzer's reverence for life and the demands he made of morality. In a way that I find highly compatible, Schweitzer wrote that reverence for life is not required to explain the significance moral people's influences have on the preservation, development and elevation of life in the general process of world events.

In comparison with the persistent and colossal natural forces bent on its destruction, the forces working to protect and perfect life are insignificant. But, Schweitzer insists, this must not discourage reverence for life. He added that, for the world, the significant thing is that, having become a moral creature, the human being manifests the will to life, a will replete with reverence for and willing self-sacrifice in the name of life.

In our era, the threat of self-destruction challenges morality. The New Thinking is your answer—the Russian answer—to the challenge.

Gorbachev: Even at an earlier date, it was already clear that, unless we halted the arms race and resolved disagreements among nuclear powers, catastrophe for all humankind would be inescapable. The world had arrived at a perilous brink. Any serious political collision could spark a nuclear war in which socialism, capitalism, and all ideological preferences and passions would go up in smoke. Our approach embodied realism and the understanding that we are all equal in the face of nuclear death. It had not yet, however, become the New Thinking as a new philosophy.

There was only one way out: to trust our eyes and call things by their real names. We had to admit the priority of life over theory, choose life, submit ourselves to its logic, and cease deceiving ourselves.

Ikeda: Religion confronts the same problems. It cannot exist outside time and life. To survive, religions must remain in close touch with life and the world. They must therefore be constantly reforming and growing. In this connection, the nature of the means we employ acquires enormous significance. How shall we follow the path of life without sacrificing the eternal and sacred in the name of the frivolous? Intellectuals for whom religion is not a profound faith remain aloof from the ordinary people who must work to earn their daily bread. Instead of understanding and drawing closer to them, they look down on their flocks' ignorance. Gabriel Marcel aptly remarked that the French political theorist Proudhon hit the mark when he called the intelligentsia frivolous. Fundamentally this is true, Marcel said, because, unlike workers and peasants who overcome a contrary reality, members of the intelligentsia work only with words, which paper receives uncritically. The decision to break with ideology and turn to realism takes great courage, I think.

Gorbachev: For us the New Thinking started with the recognition of what was evident and indisputable; that is, that socialism and capitalism are only different alternatives on the path of the development of human civilization. But the recognition of the world's essential heterogeneity and of diversity of values and means was only the first step. The second, which derives from the first, was recognition of the essential interconnections and mutual interdependence of everything in the world.

Ikeda: Your words hark back to the Buddhist conception of dependent origination as the source of all existence. Obviously, phenomena have particular meanings. But individual traits can manifest themselves in their full glory only because of the universal interconnectedness of existence.

This extremely dynamic viewpoint resonates with your ideas of the essential interconnection and interdependence of the world. Because of this interconnection, coexistence is the key to the essence of the 21st century.

Gorbachev: The interdependence of the world was by no means our discovery. It has existed in all developed philosophical systems, including dialectical materialism. Nonetheless, the idea had never before been used to evaluate real cooperation between two social systems; that is, real cooperation between socialism and capitalism without biased evaluations of the roles and perspectives of liberal and socialist theories. In the world at large and in specific nations, both systems have expressed the interests of various social strata. In the past, rupture, confrontation, and the exclusive nature of one or the other had always been the focal point. In our breakthrough shift to the New Thinking, we limited ourselves to the minimum by searching for real cooperation between socialism and capitalism and discerning its place in world history.

A novel departure for its time, the recognition of diverse starting mechanisms for civilizational development opened new perspectives for internal politics, too, and revealed new possibilities for greater progress.

In the USSR, the restoration of general human values and simple moral norms inevitably led to the rehabilitation of the church as a mechanism of personal spiritual development and restraint of innate egoism. Rehabilitation of capitalism as an alternative economic approach led to the rehabilitation of the market, of market–money relations, enterprise, and economic activity. This too was a real breakthrough in communist ideology, which, like medieval Catholicism, persecuted morally and philosophically the very idea of enterprise and market culture. Our view inevitably stimulated a reinterpretation of the essence of international

relations and international politics. We envisioned not merely cooperation and coexistence, but also the application of positive experience and
mechanisms for preserving and realizing humanity-wide values. This
was, of course, verification of conditions that exist in life itself.

This approach helped us discover the true meaning of humanity-
wide values in international relations. Good faith, mutual respect, the
spirit of partnership, and trust became essential conditions for the new
diplomacy. The world has become so small and so interrelated and
interdependent that no one country or government can defend its own
interests and security unilaterally. Thus the idea of collective responsibility—especially on the part of the USSR and the USA—for the fate
of humanity and civilization gradually came to play a larger and larger
role in external politics.

The New Thinking stimulated us to seek a way to overcome not only
class and ideological schism, but also racial, religious, and economic
schism throughout the world. The idea behind the effort was simple and
universally accessible. The more we quarrel and clash, the more new
fissures appear in the walls and perhaps in the foundations of the world.

Ikeda: In other words, the New Thinking constituted a return to good
sense. But why had the Russian people been content to live split lives
for such a long time? On the one hand, they existed within the official
ideological framework; on the other, they followed the dictates of
elementary good sense. Be that as it may, however, good sense
triumphed in the end.

Gorbachev: That is right. The Russians had always manifested the
elementary instinct of self-preservation. As the old saying goes: "Don't
saw off the branch you're sitting on." The crossover to good sense had
great consequences.

The New Thinking enabled us to rebuild the entire structure of our
international relations, both in terms of policies of the Central
Committee and at the governmental level. First we extended the hand
of reconciliation to the social-democrats. Opposition between the
socialist and the capitalist paths to development became meaningless.
Even more anachronistic than the socialist–capitalist standoff, however,
had been opposition between revolutionary and reforming tendencies
within the international workers' movement.

We found ourselves compelled to reexamine the already entrenched
view of the social-democrats as renegades and of ourselves as the only
successors to its great labor-movement traditions. History showed that
each side had its weaknesses, its positive aspects, its mistakes, and its

indisputable successes and achievements. Grain by grain, the theory and practice of the New Thinking took shape.

Ikeda: Although younger generations perhaps cannot grasp it, the decision to be reconciled with the social-democrats made excellent sense. Smashing the social-democrats had been Stalin's idea. But Lenin's guard too played a big part. The Bolsheviks considered themselves to be the only heirs to Marxism, the only executors of the will of the proletarian revolution. Any opponent was an enemy. Any weak or potentially harmful element must be ruthlessly exposed. Resource to violence is acceptable if necessary. Blows to the enemy must be merciless. This entire strategy reduces the human being to nothing but a means to political aims.

Gorbachev: Actually the destructive outcomes of the Stalinist struggle with the social-democrats have long been known—even since the time of the Khrushchev thaw. At the beginning of the 1960s, in his film *Ordinary Fascism (Obyknovennyi fashism)*, Mikhail Romm told the Soviet moviegoer how the Comintern made enemies of the social-democrats, thus causing a schism in the German workers' movement as a result of which Hitler was able to come to power. In his own relations with the social-democrats Stalin adhered to the sadistic formula, "Beat the folks at home so the folks abroad will fear you".

When we reformers came to power, we established justice and rectified a decades-old situation by normalizing relations with the social-democrats.

Ikeda: Mahatma Gandhi criticized the Bolshevik belief that the end justifies the means. What are your opinions of his philosophy of non-violence? He condemned revolutionary, violent socialism. Feeling that socialism must be as pure as crystal, he insisted that all means toward its attainment, too, must be crystal-pure: unclean methods discredit goals and defeat causes.

Gorbachev: The moral spirit of Perestroika rejected the idea that the end justifies the means. In this sense, our purification from Bolshevik amoralism followed a path laid down in his time by Mahatma Gandhi himself.

But the concept of national security was the most important aspect of the theory and practice of the New Thinking. Within its framework, we had to discover how to ensure our own security and lift the threat of nuclear self-destruction. To the militaristic doctrine founded on the politics of force, we opposed the concept of balanced interests and mutual, equal security. Our recognition of the growing role in world affairs of still-forming nations necessitated taking into consideration diversity of interests and free choice. This, too, was an important element in the New Thinking.

In the course of analyzing fundamental global changes, we overcame many of the stereotypes that had fettered our options. My own extensive contacts with representatives of other countries included heads of state and ordinary citizens; universally acknowledged authorities in science and culture; outstanding writers; leaders and delegates of political parties, social organizations and movements; and union and social-democrat leaders, religious figures, and parliamentarians. These contacts, too, played a big role. Indeed, this saturation of direct contact seems to have reintroduced the Soviet Union to the outside world. From our viewpoint, it became possible for us to see and understand the world better, to participate in discussions of its problems and searches for solutions, and to extract useful ideas from different cultures and spiritual traditions. All of this vitalized Soviet external policies and enabled us to advance a whole series of large-scale initiatives—for instance, the program for stage-by-stage liquidation of nuclear arms by 2000, the concept of the Common European Home, and reconstruction of relations in the Asia–Pacific region.

Our sincere and open invitation to think matters over together and seek solutions stimulated great response worldwide. And Glasnost and Perestroika gave material cogency to our foreign political ideas and initiatives.

Ikeda: You say that the world seems to have been reintroduced to the Soviet Union. Frankly, I too felt a new familiarity with your country. As a Buddhist, I consider the human being more important than the system and adhere to the opinion that it is possible to engage in dialogue with the members of a society no matter what its political structure. That is why, true to my convictions, I go on making constant contact with people of many countries and developing folk diplomacy to the full extent of my capability. But it is very difficult to overcome dissimilar governmental positions and differences in social systems in order to engage in direct person-to-person dialogue. This is especially true with politicians, in dealing with whom possibilities for dialogue immediately and noticeably narrow.

You are a rare exception. When, after our first meeting in 1990, a Japanese journalist asked me what impression you had made on me, I replied, "His soul is open to dialogue. With him it's always possible to find a common language."

Top state leaders bear the responsibility for the future of humanity. My long-standing dream is for them to engage in dialogue and sincere open discussions that can eliminate the mutual isolation between conflicting political systems. You were the first to make a big step toward the realization of my dream.

Gorbachev: Through your missionary activities, you have proved the possibility of engaging in dialogue about peace and of reinforcing popular diplomacy even under Iron Curtain conditions. At our meeting in Tokyo, in April, 1993, you impressed me greatly by describing how, as early as the 1960s, at the height of the Cold War, your party worked to establish diplomatic relations between Japan and China. I know you were criticized for this initiative. But you won. Or, more precisely, the truth of history triumphed. The Cold War was contrary to the interests of humanity.

Even in the early years of Perestroika, politicians who embraced the New Thinking produced notable positive results. First of all, relationships between the Soviet Union and the United States improved. Withdrawal of Soviet forces from Afghanistan was an international landmark strengthening faith in new Soviet policies. At the same time it provided impetus for the regulation of regional conflicts.

Of course, the reasons for the rending of human civilization turned out to be deeper and more serious than we foresaw while formulating the New Thinking. In itself, the abrogation of ideological conflict did not lead automatically to a general, definitive peace. Certainly, the threat of nuclear catastrophe lessened. But a considerable number of threats that we had not taken into consideration emerged.

The Cold War froze numerous geopolitical, national, and ethnic conflicts, not all of which were connected to the Cold War itself. Some were inherited from the past, even from the 19th and early 20th centuries. The Cold War quasi-stability created a reassuring impression that the post-conflict world order was predictable.

But when the anesthetic of the Cold War wore off, many heretofore concealed disputes burst forth. Some assumed the form of conflicts, armed skirmishes, or governmental collapse. The new instability, the spreading of bloody conflicts, and the inability of international institutions to check them sharply worsened the general psychological world atmosphere. Depression, pessimism, gloomy prophecies and premonitions, corruption, callousness in the face of the daily violent deaths of hundreds and thousands of people, the emergence of shocking refugee problems—all these phenomena created a breeding ground for corruption, terrorism, drug trafficking, contraband, and widespread violations of laws and civilized rules of behavior.

Ikeda: You are right. The triumph of liberal over communistic values spawned new, intractable trials. The same arrogance, the same superficial attitude towards problems and difficulties persist in the post-Cold War world. We still have the same notorious double standards: what is permitted to the strong is denied to the weak. The result of all this is a new, not Bolshevik, but liberal moral chaos, uncertainty in everything, and fear of the future. Today's spiritual situation reminds me of the plague described in the nightmares of the convict Raskolnikov in Dostoyevsky's *Crime and Punishment*. He dreams that the whole world is condemned to be sacrificed to a fearsome, unprecedented pestilence arriving in Europe from the depths of Asia. Everybody except a chosen few must perish. The new microscopic trichinae taking up residence in the human body are actually spirits endowed with mind and will. People infested with them immediately become possessed and run mad. Ironically, however, the infested feel supremely wise and steadfast in the truth. The tragedy of the post-Cold War epoch resembles this weird plague. People consider themselves wise in spite of raging wars, senseless sacrifices, and the same old fear. As Dostoyevsky wrote, "They vow never to part. Then immediately they began doing something different from what they had just proposed: they began blaming each other."

How can we free ourselves from this chaos? I should be interested to hear your opinion of the new moral plague. Even in the face of it, you remain optimistic. What is the source of your optimism?

Gorbachev: Please do not interpret what I say as an argument for the return of the Cold War with its imperatives for internal and international discipline. On the contrary, my remarks are further proof of the enormous damage the Cold War did. The simultaneous defeat of the Fascist powers in 1945 provided a unique chance to pursue a different path. But the Cold War turned our steps along a vicious vector.

What now? The only option I see is to deepen and develop the fundamental moral bases of the philosophy we call the New Thinking. What follows from the global interconnectedness of the world? First of all, the need for peoples and governments to accept responsibility for each other. No one is permitted to solve their own problems at the cost of somebody else. Today's generations have no right to find happiness and well-being at the expense of their progeny.

Ikeda: Although we met only twice, I was deeply sympathetic when I saw you on the television screen on your return from house arrest in the Crimea, after the leaders of the putsch had been defeated, an exhausted president who clearly found it difficult to maintain his distinctive Gorbachev smile.

Gorbachev: When I think back over the terrible days of August 1991, I find strength in the thought that the events connected with the attempted coup and the so-called State Emergency Committee behind it are some of the most tragic moments of 20th-century Russian history.

Please understand that I am not talking about myself and my private fate, although those were the most difficult days—even minutes—of my life as a human being and as a politician.

Ikeda: Everything occurring in those days revealed the nature of human beings like a Greek or a Shakespearian tragedy. I make this comment because even today many superficial and silly rumors persist about you and Perestroika. For instance, a number of people claim that your art of balancing between right and left, thus ensuring your own security, failed you. Some even suspect you of behind-the-scenes participation in the coup. How did you feel at the time? What is your psychological state now?

Gorbachev: For me, the tragedy was that, after dealing the coup leaders a decisive blow on August 18 by rejecting their ultimatum, I was unable to stay in power and continue the reforms I had started. But, even if I had known beforehand what would happen after the defeat of the hard-line coup—the disintegration of the Soviet Union, the setting up of the Commonwealth of Independent States, and endless betrayals by my companions—I still would not have made a deal with the coup leaders. As a politician and a man in that extreme, classically existential situation, I depended on and was oriented to fundamental values: duty, the constitution, law, and—for me—democracy. To betray democracy and choose violence would have meant spiritual and probably political suicide.

Response to a new challenge in a situation like that is a spontaneous impulse of will. There is no thought of fear. When you are in a totally new situation, the keenness of your impressions masks fear. My first thought was how should I act, what decision should I take? I realized that I was faced with a new mission unlike any I had ever dealt with. I told the people near and dear to me that we faced something serious. I said to Raisa Maksimovna, Irina, and Anatoliy that I would not retreat from my position and absolutely would not give in to blackmail, threats, or pressure.

Ikeda: To tell the truth, few Western politicians would be willing to relinquish power to demonstrate their loyalty to democratic values. As a rule, it is impossible to give power back. That is why the choice you made then has a truly existential character. You went counter to human nature and to the nature of power in the tradition of Russian political culture. No one before in Russia had ever sacrificed power in the name of democratic values. One wonders whether the new leaders can demonstrate your loyalty to democratic ideals. Those values seldom correspond to the routine of democratic procedures. This too defines your drama. Within the framework of an established system, democracy is relative and is occupied with adjusting interests and reaching compromises.

Gorbachev: Like you, I think we must distinguish between the political and moral contents of democracy. Unfortunately, Russians today mistake the technology of democracy—democratic procedures, elections, and referenda—for its essence. Of course, things like direct, free, fair elections and the principle of the division of power are important. More important still, however, is the idea of the initial spiritual equality of all people. That lies at the very foundation of democracy. It is important for each person to learn to identify with others and to realize that everyone's life is unique and that we all share the same interests. We must realize that everybody wants to be happy and to experience the joys of human existence. Anyone who deeply feels this equality is a true democrat.

You ask how I reacted to betrayal on the part of people I had trusted. To speak honestly, in the days of the attempted coup, nothing hit me as hard as the treachery of people who had been at my side for many years and who—like General Plekhanov, chief of the guard, and Marshal Yazov, minister of defense—were indebted to me. What they did was hard to imagine. The betrayal by Lukyanov, a comrade from school days, was the hardest blow.

Ikeda: I can imagine. Although in ordinary situations and not on the scene of world history, as in your case, I too have run up against betrayal and treachery several times. Because it undermines trust—one of the noblest aspects of the human spirit—treachery is unforgivable.

Gorbachev: After the trials of the past few years, I now take a calm view of the betrayals of those days in August. They were dreadful, but worse still were the vile, foul lies about the events produced by both our new-Stalinists and our brilliant "Democrats".

In spite of the tragedy, everything was simple in August 1991. Champions of democratic reform stood up against the reactionary enemies of change. One side refused to accept Perestroika and democratic reforms and, counting most of all on popular dissatisfaction, took criminal steps. In a crucial moment in Russian history, the other side rose up in defense of democracy, the constitution, and legal power. Ironically, however, many who defended democracy and Moscow's White House actually betrayed the interests of democracy. This has nothing to do with Yeltsin. Gavril Popov's belated admission that Yeltsin did not so much save Gorbachev as implement a contrived plan for getting him out of the way was no news. Tragically, the same people who defended the White House in 1991 fired on it in 1993. People who, I thought, had democratic convictions proved false to the interests and values of democracy. Now they call for the setting up of an authoritarian regime in Russia and insult people who were once with them.

Ikeda: On a smaller scale, Japan underwent political changes a few years ago. Thirsting for power, political groups that had been as incompatible as oil and water for over forty years suddenly joined hands. I refrain from making judgments about whether the old system was better than the new. Undeniably, however, as a consequence of this sudden coming together of ideological enemies, the people now entertain hopeless contempt for everything political. Politicians glibly manipulate words and tailor them to their own aims. They are capable of limitlessly altering their principles and their mottos and of breaking their promises without a qualm. They ignore their fellow citizens or the millions of people who entrusted power to them.

Among the ordinary people, cynicism breeds cynicism; distrust fosters distrust. This creates the atmosphere of disappointment with democratic procedures that, as a rule, leads to authoritarianism and dictatorship.

And this all happens when spiritual life and interests wither. A Russian intellectual friend of mine commented on the lack of extremely popular writers in Moscow today. Everyone is satisfied with prosaic, everyday interests, and no one is concerned about the heights of the human spirit. Paradoxically, in this connection, the era of party censorship was distinguished by great attention to spiritual matters. Whereas I by no means recommend a return to the past, this seems to me to indicate a current spiritual crisis.

Ortega y Gasset was afraid of societies ruled, not by the spirit, but by standardized mass opinions and evaluations propagated every minute by electronic means of communication, most of all by television. Is Russia going to be the next victim of the omnipotent mass media?

Gorbachev: Your highly topical question touches the essence of the drama unfolding today in Russia. It worries me as a professional politician and as a citizen. The politicization of social life helps rot its spiritual foundation. Two questions arise in this connection. Are we Russians paying too high a price for our first experience of democracy? Is there no other, less painful way to democratize the nation? When we started Perestroika, we believed that free elections in the center and in the regions would bring to power wise, honest people who cared about the general good.

Nothing of the kind occurred. The quality of social administration is no better than it was. Responsibility and professionalism have diminished. Never has officialdom been as morally rotten as now. Understanding the events of August 1991 takes us to the depths of Russian history. It makes us understand the difference between true and sham patriotism, between real and sham democracy. It makes us think about the primordial tragic elements of history, with all its missed chances and irreparable losses.

The State Emergency Committee was responsible for frustrating the signing of the new Union Treaty of Federation. Although it was the only real alternative to the disintegration of the nation, it aborted. And the people responsible for the coup did their utmost to convince the Russian people of their patriotism.

After the events of August, all the republics announced their independence within a few days. What happened in those tragic times alienated from Moscow, the historical capital, many peoples and provoked nationalistic passions. The signing of the treaty would have guaranteed reasonable political balance between the interests of the republics and those of the center.

My main political and—if you like—moral task as president of the USSR was to preserve, renew, and reform the Union. All my aspirations were concentrated on preserving unity. I found support in the will of the people expressed by an overwhelming majority in a referendum.

The 1991 coup headed by neo-Stalinists pushed society into the arms of demagogues calling for a "final, decisive battle". The treaty setting up the Commonwealth of Independent States (CIS) followed on the heels of the State Emergency Committee. Then came the so-called shock therapy and a new, violent, Russian revolution from the top. Russia blew up. And not only Russia.

Ikeda: I vividly remember seeing you on television in the streets of Vilnius persuading people to live in amity. Some will say you were right, others will say differently. Nonetheless, as I watched, I had the sense of being a witness at the birth of the very spirit of "soft power".

Reckless power lust and passion for profit seem to have triumphed temporarily. But, in the long view, the flow of time will wash away superfluities; and in the end the people you talk about will be seen to have dug their own graves.

Gorbachev: Therein lies the tragic drama of human existence. Sooner or later the principle of moral retribution, the principle of justice, takes effect. For example, the ultimate condemnation in Russia of the murderers of Tsar Nicholas II and his family had enormous significance for the moral education of the Russian nation. But when? After seventy years! History flows according to its own laws. Moral life flows according to a time that is measured on various scales. The phases of insight here do not coincide.

CHAPTER THREE

Humanity, Faith, and Religion

Basic Human Values

Gorbachev: Mr Ikeda, you are a philosopher and a religious leader. In this part of our dialogue, I want to discuss the role and place of religion and the religious value system on which to build a new civilization.

The present era is a time of great ordeal for Russian young people. The epoch in which they live and grow is one of immense breakup. Old, mostly communist, values have become impotent; and new values are not yet making themselves fully heard. In the past, young people knew clearly what to pursue and what to avoid. Greater career opportunities and better chances to live well were open to better students. Soviet society was very much like feudal society. The nearly transparent ladder to prestige was visible from all sides—from the simple field hand to the kolkhoz manager, from the subordinate worker to the foreman, from the junior laboratory assistant to the professor or academician, and, finally, from the district committee secretary to the Secretary of the Central Committee of the Communist Party of the Soviet Union. Everything was clear. Though personal connections played a significant part, talent and hard work were essential.

Today, young people find choosing role models hard. Few of them want to devote themselves to science—especially the study of fundamental sciences like mathematics, physics, and chemistry—when many outstanding scientists drag out wretched existences and when thousands of highly qualified engineers are out of work.

The so-called New Russians are pursuing wild careers. A person with a new idea becomes a millionaire in a year. People gamble on success and adventurism but not on work, knowledge, and moral values. A few lose hundreds of thousands of dollars in the casinos of Paris and London, while thousands—millions—of talented workers struggle under enormous burdens. This contrast has a highly negative influence on young people.

But the situation is not hopeless. Young people prize democracy and the freedoms they have obtained and will never want to return to the totalitarian past. True, they cause trouble. Permissiveness makes them go bad. They become part of the criminal scene. Drug abuse is getting worse, and juvenile criminal behavior has risen sharply.

Nonetheless, many young people use the blessing of freedom for spiritual and intellectual development and for self-realization. They have learned to protect their dignity. They are sincere in their attainments, in their sympathies and antipathies. In recent years, meeting young students in Saint Petersburg, Moscow, Novgorod, and the cities of Siberia and the Volga region has become one of my greatest enjoyments. Such encounters are always spiritual holidays for me. These young people seem to me to be real Gorbachev-ites—that is, advocates of democracy and good sense.

But it is perilous to predict. Not long after the velvet revolution in Czechoslovakia and the other successful revolutions in Eastern Europe, the Yugoslavia catastrophe started, and fires of war began raging across the immense post-communism expanse. Then came outbreaks of racism and nationalism in Germany and Western Europe. We in Russia are living through the disaster of war in Chechnya.

Ikeda: Your experience with the transition from communist dogma to democracy has immense significance for an understanding of the complex core values of contemporary Western civilization. In many respects, liberal values—freedom most of all—are interpreted as a blessing, in contrast to the values of communist totalitarianism—subservience, total uniformity, cruel collectivization, and sacrifice in the name of a future paradise on earth. But, as your personal experience shows, individual freedom is pregnant with contradictions. Liberty and a total break with communist social ways and unifying restrictions have diverse consequences. As you say, they can create the conditions under which the individual reaches his or her prime and finds a place in contemporary civilization. For many, however, they can become stimuli for demoralization; self-destruction of the individual; and the severance of all social ties uniting the individual with the family, society, and the nation.

By its very nature, freedom presupposes egocentrism. There is no great harm in this, as long as it does not lead to cynicism and flagrant cupidity. To their great grief, the former socialist nations began returning to European civilization just in time for the profound moral crisis of the epoch of so-called double moral standards, the hallmark of which is the preeminence of personal concerns at the expense of other values, hedonism, power, and greed.

Gorbachev: You have brought up a problem that disturbs me very much. Today, quite rightly and justly, much is said about the failure of communist messianism. But contemporary Western bourgeois civilization cannot necessarily provide spiritual guidelines for the future. Today's Western civilization is sick. Its characteristic vices are extreme individualism, cupidity—which you just mentioned—commercialism, and dependence. In Russia, our current attempts to become European fast and to set out on the path of modern civilization have so far led only to an explosion of commercialism and the race to "get rich quick" at any cost. The struggle with vulgar collectivism has led only to vulgar individualism. Do we have what it takes to realize our expectations of the new century? Do we have enough moral and physical strength— enough wisdom—to withstand new trials?

Perestroika in the ideological sphere began with a departure from the class approach to morality. Life itself and the logic of Soviet history led us to a simple truth: there is only one true morality. Bourgeois and prole-tarian morality cannot exist simultaneously. Considerations of a practical nature propelled us toward such a conclusion. Without a single morality, there can be no single system of values. Without a single system of values, we have no chance for dialogue, therefore cannot expect to overcome opposition between social systems of capitalism and communism.

Ikeda: Reforms always begin with spiritual reformation. The greatness of Perestroika is that it started precisely with a reexamination of moral values and the need for everything to be ruled by criteria common to all humanity. Positioning human life at the apex, it rejected classifying morality as bourgeois or proletarian. Although specific reforms may succeed or fail, the universal and historical significance of Perestroika is unquenchable. It demonstrated the limitless moral strengths of the peoples of the USSR—what I would call their spiritual durability, their capability of moral self-purification after long years of Stalinism. They overcame the heritage of totalitarian ideology within themselves.

Without religion, morality lacks life force. Without a religious under-standing of the place of humanity in the universe, morality is like a tree with no soil in which to sink its roots. I assign the broadest meaning to religion, with no reference to specific creeds. When I say "religion", I am talking about core universal human values enabling us to tell good from bad.

Since man does not live by bread alone, this distinction is of para-mount importance. Human beings experience spiritual as well as physical hunger. Consciously or not, the truly human being always senses the need to comprehend the meaning of life. Such comprehen-sion is impossible without knowledge of what is supreme. Religion has value because it reminds us of the existence of something higher than finite human life and its vanity. It reminds us of the oneness of death and immortality. The pangs of conscience intimate the existence of the Eternal and teach us that there is something more important and valuable than transitory egotistical interests.

How is it possible to call a society humane and prosperous if its citizens live exclusively for the sake of daily bread? Can the citizens of such a society consider themselves happy if they know nothing in life except cutthroat competition? In the final reckoning, spiritual impoverishment desiccates our sources of creativity with inevitable effects on society's material development.

As the foundation of a general system of values, religion cannot and must not be confined within the narrow frame of the metaphysical world. Soul, or spiritual condition, reflects in everything a person does, creates, or comes into contact with. Life cannot be evaluated solely on either the material or the ideal plane. Both components are organically connected. Consequently, we must admit the deciding role faith plays in both spiritual and material development.

Viewing it within too narrow a scope, our contemporaries in East and West alike identify religion with rites and ceremonies. The non-churchgoer who believes in no divine powers can nonetheless be deeply religious. Religion can be defined as the cosmological outlook determining the mutual relation between the universe and the human being and the moral principles that serve as behavior criteria. A person who knows where he is and where he is headed in this infinite universal space already has a religion. To discover its nature, we must examine our being not only in the present, but also in the past and the future. That is why faith is related to an understanding of what awaits the human being after death.

In a way, giving priority to the material over the spiritual is a kind of religion. No conviction has exhaustive proofs. We must therefore admit that we do not always truly know something but only believe in it, without significant evidence.

The human being cannot live without faith. It is as necessary as air. But we never think about the invisible air until we find breathing hard. As Fyodor Dostoevsky said: "Even with plenty of money, a society collapses if it lacks noble ideas" (Fyodor Mikhailovich Dostoyevsky, *Sekai Bungaku Zenshu 44*, Collected World Literary Works, Vol. 44 [Tokyo: Kodansha, 1977], p.178). His words sound like the pain of lungs that have been deprived of air. Having lost ideals rooted in the life-giving soil of faith, many people wonder why their souls are in pain.

In my view, it is senseless to ask whether we need faith. We need only seek an object of faith. Lev Tolstoy wrote in "What Is My Faith?" that the religion of unreligious people consists in obeying the powers that be; that is, in doing whatever the majority does.

Many Japanese today consider it wise to have no definite faith. They, therefore, become entrapped by false commercial prophets hiding behind the mask of occultism or claiming to serve truth. This sad tendency arises among us because, never having passed through thorny ideological quests, the Japanese people remain obedient to authority and have lost the will and the desire to know the truth. After all, it is easier to submit and follow the path of the majority than to travel the agonizing way of the quest for truth and spiritual perfection. Stupefied by material blessings, many fail even to notice their own wretched spiritual condition.

The human being cannot live without an object of faith. Those who do not believe in the infinite turn to the finite. Those who feel no reverence before the invisible, secret force of life are likely to become prisoners to visible secular power. The person in a position of power considers himself an omnipotent lord and confines himself within the narrow frame of his own limited reason.

At one time, the Japanese government foisted off State Shinto on the Japanese people as the sole official religion. For their refusal to recognize this politically motivated religion, Tsunesaburo Makiguchi, first president of Soka Gakkai, and Josei Toda, second president, were imprisoned. Mr Toda, my mentor, was released after two years; Mr Makiguchi died in prison. In those days, opposition to the militarists meant death. But, as lay followers of the Buddhism of Nichiren Daishonin, Mr Makiguchi and Mr Toda were unafraid because their firm faith was an inexhaustible source of spiritual strength. The clergy of the Nichiren sect, on the other hand, obediently and slavishly abandoned their own faith in favor of the official one.

False religion, political power, and the mass-information media— which during World War II obediently abandoned their own convictions and supported the state-glorifying religion—provoked military expansion in Asia. These elements constitute the Japanese establishment to the present day.

At heart, the religious apathy reigning in Japan is not atheism, but a nationalistic faith that still prevents the Japanese from being honest with the rest of the world.

After pressure from Western nations forced her to open her boundaries in the latter half of the 19th century, Japan employed nationalist ideals as a means of self-defense against Western imperialism. By transforming an ancient indigenous religion into State Shinto, the nationalists were able to concoct a kind of cement to hold the people together. In this way, religion became nationalism. Of course, nationalism is itself a kind of faith.

The outstanding English historian Arnold J. Toynbee once told me that the spiritual vacuum left in Europe after Christianity lost its effective power in the 17th century was filled by three religions—science, nationalism, and communism. All three of them aim to satisfy cupidity and the thirst for material blessings in contrast to ancient religious ideals of self-control and the constraint of greed.

Christianity and Communism

Gorbachev: At the Gorbachev Foundation, we are interested in discovering which values have justified themselves in relation to civilization and which have outlived their usefulness. Here I am speaking specifically about the relation between Communism and Christianity. Are the same principles of equality to be found at the heart of both?

Lev Tolstoy—whom no one could call a socialist—assumed that the idea of universal equality lies at the foundation of Christianity and of all religions in general. In "I Believe", he wrote: "Christianity proclaims equality not as the outcome of relations between human beings and the infinite, but as a foundation for a doctrine of the brotherhood of all peoples, since all are recognized as children of God."

But, for Christianity to grow stronger, the idea of universal equality too had to gain strength. Does Communism contain ideas more important than that of equality? After all, many thinkers claim that primitive Christianity was a form of Communism. Does the idea of Communist equality offer perspectives useful to the 21st century? Can religious ideology supplant socialism and Communism completely?

In this connection arises the question of the parallel roles of Marx and Christ in history. Can we consider Christ to have been a forerunner of Marx? After all Marx, too, warned against laying up treasures on earth. Christ, on the other hand, said: "Think not that I am come to send peace on earth: I came not to send peace, but a sword. For I am come to set a man at variance against his father" (Matthew 10:34–35).

Ikeda: Christianity and Communism share many things in common—universal equality, prohibition of private property, messianism, and so on. That is why Communism is sometimes called a shadow religion or the religion that replaced Christianity. The affinity between the two took a more radical form in Russia than in other European countries. Nikolai Berdyaev concentrated his attention on the similarity. He wrote that Communist power, too, is concerned with saving the souls of its adherents and instructing them in the unique saving truth. It knows the truth—the truth of dialectical materialism. From the Christian position, many clergymen have indicted private property in ways so radical as to surprise even socialists like Marx and Proudhon, who consider private property the source of all evil.

Gorbachev: You believe that the idea of equality in one form or another has always been part of religion. If so, why has it not been more prominent? Why have the devotees of cults—and this pertains to all religions—not complied with it in life? Why do they still not comply with it?

Ikeda: Precisely because they have not and do not, the socialists were and are able to play a messianic role in place of the church and to concentrate attention on the poor and the outcast. Communism protects equality in distribution and in the rights of societal life. But I think it is more important still to concentrate on the meaning of the human being under conditions of universal equality.

Dostoyevsky's ideas on the topic are interesting. The hero of *The Possessed*, a revolutionary schemer, says: "They're all slaves and equal in slavery... There must be equality in the herd... Leveling mountains is a good idea." But equality that regards human society as a flock of impotent sheep inevitably leads first to egalitarianism and then to slavery and totalitarianism.

But the idea of equality can incorporate various approaches to humanity. Some claim we are all equal because we are all the children of sin. Others, on the other hand, regard the human being as a unique datum and consider us all equal in this sense.

Gorbachev: These quests for the nature and roots of values common to all compelled Russian atheists and Marxists to reread the Sermon on the Mount. Can we think that it concentrates all human wisdom? Can we equate Judeo-Christian values with those of all humanity? I ask out of the desire to avoid making new idols for myself—out of the wish to understand what the East of today can contribute to the trove of universal human values. Perhaps there is only one religion—one humanity-wide wisdom expressed in diverse words.

Suppose that you and I were called upon to create a new Sermon on the Mount. As a representative of Buddhism and of other Eastern religions, what would you add to what Christ said?

Ikeda: You have set me an extraordinary task. Probably I would not add anything to the Sermon on the Mount. Instead I would answer your question in the following way. The person whose life embodies the Sermon on the Mount is not only a real Christian, but also a real Buddhist. Buddhism does not classify people according to their religious associations. It concentrates not on religious confession, but on individual behavior, which in Buddhist terminology means deeds, words, and thoughts. In practical terms, the basic aim of Buddhism is to direct all thought and action toward the creation of beauty, good, and happiness.

Consequently, a person who is a Buddhist on paper may be far from a Buddhist in behavior, and vice-versa. Nichiren Daishonin once wrote of wise men who lived before his time, "And though the adherents of the non-Buddhist scriptures were unaware of it, the wisdom of such men contained at heart the wisdom of Buddhism" (*WND*, p. 1122). Buddhism is tolerant of external differences because it prizes only a person's spirit and deeds.

The Sermon on the Mount and Buddhist teachings have much in common. For instance, in the Gospel according to Matthew, we read: "Blessed are ye, when [men] shall revile you, and persecute [you], and shall say all manner of evil against you falsely, for my sake" (Matthew 5:11). Nichiren Daishonin, too, speaks of spiritual elevation as a result of the persecutions that the believer cannot escape: "... difficulties will arise, and these are to be looked on as 'peaceful' practices" (*The Record of the Orally Transmitted Teachings* [Tokyo: Soka Gakkai, 2004], p. 115).

The Sermon on the Mount teaches, "That you may be the children of your Father which art in heaven: for he maketh his sun to rise on the evil and on the good, and sendeth rain on the just and on the unjust" (Matthew 5:45). In the Lotus Sutra, the supreme Buddhist scripture, there is a passage: "the Law preached by the Buddha is comparable to a great cloud which, with a single-flavored rain, moistures human flowers so that each is able to bear fruit" (Lotus Sutra, p. 105). In other words, the Buddhist teachings are addressed to absolutely everybody.

There are other similarities as well. Jesus says, "Beware of false prophets, which come to you in sheep's clothing, but inwardly they are ravening wolves" (Matthew 7:15). In a letter to a disciple, Nichiren Daishonin wrote a similar warning against false priests, whom he describes as animals in priestly robes (*WND*, p. 760).

Shakyamuni Buddha manifested the humanity of his teachings not only in words, but also in deeds. Once the Great Teacher personally cared for a sick man. He spread straw for him to lie on, wiped his body, and laundered his underclothes. He then told his disciples: "Look after this sick man. To serve a suffering person is the same thing as serving the Buddha." In effect, the Buddha himself served the Buddha by being compassionate to a suffering being. In this sense, the "Buddha" to be served is human life itself. People who cultivate their sense of humanity and constantly seek self-perfection through serving and guarding life are Buddhas, the highest form of humanity. Everyone is a potential Buddha. The potential is realized when we are humane in our actions. In other words, the word "Buddha" does not mean a superhuman, sacred condition endowed with a fixed status.

According to Max Weber, European religions characteristically define the human being as an instrument of God created to the glory of God. Weber considered the distinctive trait of Asiatic religions to be the idea of the human being as a vessel containing God. He pointed out these contrasts, but it is impossible to draw a clear demarcation line between them because Eastern and Western faiths both contain elements of each other.

Shakyamuni was a human being. He cautioned his followers against idealizing him. He indicated equality between himself and his followers by treating them like good friends. After his departure from life, however, some of his followers began elevating the human Shakyamuni and the concept of the Buddha to heights unattainable by ordinary people. Possibly this tendency arose from his disciples' unusually deep respect and sincere love for him. Perhaps it resulted from profound grief at being separated from him. Undeniably, however, some monks were avid to deify Shakyamuni in order to enhance their own significance at having been his close associates.

In reaction against it, some people began advocating a return to the initial teaching of respect for all as Buddhas, thus giving rise to Mahayana Buddhism. But history shows that at still later dates, for various reasons, the tendency to absolutize the Buddha gained ground. In 13th-century Japan, having studied Mahayana teachings, Nichiren Daishonin strove to inspire a return to the founder's original ideas. He summarized this attitude in the statement: "It is thought that Shakyamuni Buddha possesses the three virtues of sovereign, teacher, and parent for the sake of all of us living beings, that is not so. On the contrary, it is common mortals who endow him with the three virtues." Bold for its time, this statement was the starting point for a transition from the subordination of human beings to religion to the subordination of religion to human beings. This is the doctrine around which the Soka Gakkai movement for absolute humanism has evolved. I suspect that similar returns to founders' fundamentals have occurred in other religions too.

Intolerance and Fanaticism

Gorbachev: Religion has coped with the ordeals that fell to its lot during the 20th century. Aggressive atheism has exhausted itself and suffered defeat.

But the question arises: Why do religious wars and conflicts occur? It would appear that all religions share the same fundamental values and are historically and genetically related. Why then do religious people today—as they did a thousand years ago—continue to go to war for their own unique deities? Why do Serbs kill each other because some of them remain Orthodox Christians while others learned Islam and became Muslims? When will the insanity of religious wars stop? Where is the tolerance that all religions recommend?

I grew up in an atheistic country where people could and usually did compromise. Why is it that ordinary people can learn tolerance in daily life while religious leaders are always picking fights? It is a known fact that all religious wars have been provoked. What separates the Catholics of Northern Ireland from the Protestants? Is there a way out? Where can we find salvation from this barbarity?

Ikeda: Yes, the question of religious tolerance and intolerance is as old as human history. The savage barbarism of religious wars is more characteristic of the monotheistic faiths like Judaism, Christianity, and Islam than of Buddhism. However, Buddhists cannot remain unconcerned observers in connection with it. I greatly appreciate the recent trend toward ecumenical dialogue and cooperation.

I categorically oppose all war. There is no justification for it, especially for religious war. For a religion, resorting to violence is tantamount to spiritual suicide. Instead of proving the superiority of its teachings, violence only exposes a religion's bankruptcy.

In connection with this firm conviction, I should like to share with you my own misgivings and doubts about the behavior of journalists who identify conflicts as wars of religion. In many cases, is it really the religions that are at conflict?

On the Balkan Peninsula and in the Near East, numerous groups professing different religions, speaking different languages, and differing in national traits live together. Many of our contemporaries are of the opinion that these peoples have been at each other's throats since time immemorial. History, however, reveals that wars in these regions have not in fact been unusually frequent. Under the Ottoman Empire, for example, these religiously diverse groups coexisted in peace. In fact, the empire was a favorite place of emigration for Jews driven out of Europe. The system of religious peaceful coexistence began to fall apart with the advent of modernism. After the collapse of the Ottoman Empire, nationalism instead of religion became the main uniting axis. Attempts to cobble together monolingual nations became widespread. But this proved to be a dangerous idea for a region inhabited by diverse ethnic groups with diverse religious beliefs. The principle of the nation state became a smoldering, sometimes explosive hotbed for conflicts. In general, these have been either national conflicts in the form of clashes of economic or material interest, or conflicts artificially ignited by power-hungry rulers. Religion has been used to justify the righteousness of this or that conflict, for psychological manipulations, and for enflaming antagonism. When this happens—as it often does—conflicts acquire a religious hue.

I am not exonerating religions of all blame. They should extinguish conflict. Unfortunately, however, an analysis of the circumstances in contemporary hotbeds of trouble demonstrates their failure to do so. Worse than impotent in warding off slaughter, religion sometimes pours oil on the flames.

There have of course been true wars of religion, but they have been less numerous than national conflicts. Having suffered the Thirty Years War, Europe created a new system of government. The Peace of Westphalia was concluded with the aim of preventing further wars of religion. It limited the right to lead forces among sovereign states. As states gained greater influence over wider areas, nationalism began attracting disintegrating religions and sects into its own system and using them for its own egoistical aims.

It is natural for human beings to want to take pride in their homelands, their nations, and their religions. Under no circumstances should this desire be violated. But many politicians and rulers have treacherously used it to inflame their citizens with hatred. When this happens, simple people are compelled to fight against each other, becoming the victims of their bloodthirsty lords.

We must not permit religion to be used in the interests of power. But latent in all kinds of power is the diabolical drive to control and manipulate. Because of its inherent acumen, religion is called upon to restrain the criminal tendency of power and to protect individual dignity. It must stand up against power that cruelly tries to make faceless ciphers of people. It must defend human dignity and the uniqueness of each human life.

You ask why omnipotent religions are incapable of overcoming the barbarity of religious war. I would answer that, paradoxically, their very omnipotence hampers them. In terms of omnipotence, the roles of God in Christianity and ideology in communist society are similar. Their goals are the same: to establish the dictatorship of an omnipotent world view. Their ambition is to extend this dictatorship not only to politics and the economy, but also to such metaphysical spheres as ideas, faith, and conscience. Two faiths battling for the spiritual world and laying claim to the unique world philosophy are bound to oppose each other. That is why Lenin naturally demonstrated both intolerance and intransigence in relation to the Church. As Berdyaev wrote, "Lenin was a passionate and convinced atheist and a hater of the Orthodox religion. He very much coarsened Marx's idea of religion, just as the followers of Lenin coarsened the ideas of Lenin himself. For Lenin, the religion problem relates exclusively to the revolutionary struggle, and its statement is adjusted to the needs of that struggle."

As to religious toleration, I should like to quote the Austrian philosopher Hans Kelsen (1881–1973). Though pessimistic, his words reveal the profound paradox of justice:

> There is no such thing as absolute justice. It defies definition. This ideal is an illusion. There are only interests and conflicts of interest and the solution of these conflicts through battle or compromise. As a matter of necessity, thoughts of peace entered the realm of rationality in place of the ideal of justice. But the necessity, and longing, for a justice that is more than mere compromise and mere peace, and, above all the belief in some kind of higher, even supreme, absolute worth are too powerful to be shaken by any rational considerations. History shows that it is simply impossible to shake this conviction. If this belief is an illusion, then it is an illusion stronger than reality. Because for most people, and perhaps even for the whole of humanity, the solution to a problem does not necessarily lie in a concept or a word. And that is also why humankind will presumably never be content with the answers of Sophists, but will again and again, be it through blood and tears, seek the path that Plato took—the path of religion. (Hans Kelsen, *Kami to Kokka: Ideologi Hihan Ronbun-shu* [Aufsätze zur Ideologiekritik], trans. Ryuichi Nagao [Tokyo: Yuhikaku, 1971], pp.107–8)

Kelsen believes that, instead of searching for truth, we should seek a compromise of human interests. But peaceful coexistence without justice is fraught with dangers. We know what peace is like under a dictatorship. The present peace under a nuclear umbrella is really no peace at all.

The principle of pluralism allows the coexistence of many interests and values. The problem is preserving the viability of a tolerant pluralistic society. After all, tolerance may be considered either acceptance of diversity or indifference. Unfortunately, we are witnesses to how cynicism grows stronger in contemporary society.

When traditional values fall apart and become relative, people may take one of two courses. First, seeing no great difference among values, they may approve of everything. Or, arguing that all is meaningless folly and nonsense, they may deny everything. In a society permeated with this cynical, egocentric mood, the spirit of wholesome criticism dies, and warm human relations collapse. The outcome can be sovereign dictatorship.

What the world today needs is honest criticism and the spirit of doubt—that is, self-knowledge. The readiness to know the essence of things and sincere dialogue enable us to avert chaos and establish true tolerance and magnanimity. In my opinion this is necessary first and foremost to us Japanese.

Various attempts are being made—for instance, in the United States—to understand the Japanese national character. Some people praise our distinctive characteristics. Others criticize us as enigmatic and incomprehensible. The range of evaluations is wide. Still the image of the Japanese as a mysterious, hard-to-understand people is apparently indelible.

Religion should lie at the basis of a people's outlook on life. In this connection, the majority of Japanese are pure pragmatists who select a religion for the given occasion—Shinto at New Year, Buddhism for funerals, and Christian church services for weddings. Many foreigners find this omnivorous approach difficult to fathom. The theologian Jan Swyngedouw, who lived in our country for many years, calls it "bag religiosity". A bag assumes the form—round or square—of whatever is put into it. This accurately and skillfully expresses Japanese syncretism, which freely takes any form or appearance.

Such a spiritual culture was advantageous as long as Japan could think only of her own development. Today, however, as integration of the global community proceeds, we must seek keys to the solutions of many problems in dialogues and associations with other cultures. We can no longer rely on traditional Japanese syncretism.

Without spiritual support and clear convictions it is absolutely impossible to win the trust of world society. It pains me to say that, with their postwar economic successes, the Japanese became arrogant and spiritually desolate. They now have no philosophy, no convictions, no ideals; all they have is immediate thrift. There are still no signs of a change in their clearly contemptuous relations with the Asiatic nations Japan once utilized in the name of her own development.

Gorbachev: Your courage astonishes me. Not everyone can speak so candidly about his homeland. Your action convinces me that the Japanese are capable not only of repentance, but also of going beyond the boundaries of history to become freer and franker towards historical truth.

Ikeda: It seems to me that tolerance has two opposed hypostases—the active and the passive. I consider active tolerance to be tolerant relations to others on the basis of love and respect for their merit. Passive tolerance is indifference and apathy. Although often interpreted as tolerance, the latter is actually worse than indifference; it is reluctance even to recognize differences. Active tolerance, on the one hand, presupposes recognition of differences. When we speak of the importance of tolerance, we must mean the word in the positive sense. We must mean relations with others arising from readiness to draw closer to each other. Such relations are rooted in love for humanity.

We must make a distinction between tolerant relations among believers and theoretical compromises. Tolerance toward other faiths does not necessarily mean religious egalitarianism, because constructive philosophical argument between different faiths need not be interpreted as intransigence. Rude or scornful relations with people of other faiths, however, are impermissible because love must be unconditional. As a Buddhist, I am convinced that people of different faiths must employ dialogue based on love and respect to strive for mutual understanding and the well-being of all humanity.

Soka Gakkai International (SGI) relies on dialogue as the most efficacious instrument for cultivating inter-people understanding. Permit me to quote from its statutes in the interests of explaining the nature of our organization:

> We believe that Nichiren Daishonin's Buddhism, a humanistic philosophy of inifinite respect for the sanctity of life and all encompassing compassion, enables individuals to cultivate and bring forth their inherent wisdom and, nurturing the creativity of the human spirit, to surmount the difficulties and crises facing humankind and realize a society of peaceful and prosperous coexistence.
>
> We, the constituent organizations and members of SGI, therefore, being determined to raise high the banner of world citizenship, the spirit of tolerance, and respect for human rights based on the humanistic spirit of Buddhism, and to challenge the global issues that face humankind through dialogue and practical efforts based on a steadfast commitment to nonviolence, hereby adopt this Charter.

Gorbachev: Faith is probably impossible without a certain sacrifice to tradition. Nikolai Berdyaev explained the psychological nature of religious faith as follows:

> The higher reason of faith reveals itself only when we take a risk, consent to the absurd, renounce our intellect, put everything on one card, and then take the leap. The reason of faith cannot reveal itself before that act of faith, that free renunciation and consent to all in the name of faith, because for it to do so would be compulsory

knowledge. Only when you prostrate yourself in the act of faith and renounce the self, can you raise yourself up and acquire a higher reason. In faith, the small individual reason disavows itself in the name of divine reason and gives itself to universal, beneficent perception. At the deepest level, faith and knowledge are one; that is, full possession of real existence.

Ikeda: Unfortunately contemporary humanity suffers from lethargy of the soul. Incapable of breakthroughs in the spiritual dimension, people lack the courage of both faith and spiritual penetration into the essence of prayer. Our epoch has forgotten prayer. We must remember that religion was born of prayer, not prayer of religion.

The praying person is humble. He is willing to be a part of the eternity he senses enveloping his life. At the risk of being misunderstood, I share with you some of my innermost thoughts on this score. I see the whole history of religious development as a history of the quest for prayer that makes possible harmonious connection with eternity and confidence in personal life.

Gorbachev: In 1993, I had the opportunity to make a report to a conference of representatives of many world religions. The occasion was outstanding in itself. Imagine Catholic archbishops, Orthodox archbishops, Islamic mullahs and rabbis all seated shoulder to shoulder in one room. It was as if all human history had come together to reconcile all times and reunite humanity. An expectation of something miraculous filled the place, as if we stood on the threshold of more important events. It was a strange situation; in many respects contradictory and difficult to explain. Perhaps this first meeting made us feel we were on the brink of a new humane community.

Ikeda: After the East European democratic revolutions, I too thought a new transformation of human existence was imminent. I felt that the epoch of animosity, violence, and oppression had passed. But these were only the illusions of romantic expectations. Both the world and the human being turned out to be more complex. The new world brought many trials, especially for the simple people, who paid a high price for democratic liberty.

The leaders of the democratic revolutions soon abandoned the masses, who had carried them to the heights of power. They started interpreting the religion of democracy in their own ways and in their own selfish interests, forgetting about the needs of the ordinary people. Russian market reforms still have not brought the longed-for prosperity.

Gorbachev: Tolstoy remarked that, with the appearance of every new religion professing universal equality, the people for whom inequality is profitable immediately and fundamentally pervert the novel teaching. This problem has a practical significance.

In Russia, thanks to Perestroika, Orthodoxy gains ground. We are glad because Orthodoxy is the religion of our forebears. We are disturbed, however, to see that revived traditions sometimes degenerate into kitsch or window-dressing devoid of spiritual content. Herein lies the danger that contemporary day-to-day civilization may ultimately undermine religion.

Ikeda: Religion remains alive as long as its growth and human spiritual development proceed side by side. As is clear from the Sermon on the Mount, the religion of Jesus Christ appeared as a protest against moribund Judaism. Jesus broke free of commandments and traditional values that were considered absolute values established by God.

In general, becoming fetters, prescriptions and rules tend to lead to alienation from humanity and therefore to the ossification and complication of human life. After this sets in, so-called authorities appear, pretending full knowledge of complicated rules used to control people. Humanity must be liberated from the tangle of ossified rules demanding subservience.

How did Christ achieve this liberation? The Sermon on the Mount clearly demonstrates his striving to transform external rules into immanent (internal) law. This is what he had in mind when he said, "Think not that I have come to destroy the law, or the prophets: I am not come to destroy, but to fulfil" (Matthew 5:17).

The Old Testament says, "Thou shalt not kill. He who kills shall be in danger of the judgment." Jesus, on the other hand says, "Whosoever is angry with his brother without a cause shall be in danger of the judgment" (Matthew 5:21). He directs his attention to anger as such. Instead of the commandment against adultery, he says, "I say unto you, That whosoever looketh on a woman to lust after her hath committed adultery with her already in his heart" (Matthew 5:28). He warns against hypocrisy in many ways. He speaks of the futility of public fasting, prayer, and religious ceremonies because he considered the internal faith behind human acts more important.

Gorbachev: Perhaps this is the secret of all religions. Their origin is not ritual, rites, and liturgy but the instinct of conscience. The conscience is not subject to any materialistic explanation. Probably it is the most important argument for the existence of a soul.

If criminal thoughts dominate him, a person can be a criminal in his soul without breaking the law. As you say, this is what Christ stressed in illuminating the intentions and ennobling the spiritual motives that control us. According to this logic, saving a person means to save his soul, to ennoble it, to preserve the person from criminal thoughts of stealing or seducing somebody's wife.

Ikeda: Very true. Goethe said that the Church ruins everything it touches. All religious people should heed his word.

In speaking of the immanence of the law, I am referring to qualities. Transforming external rules into an immanent law is to transform the imperative of God into an immanent, internal imperative directly connected with God within the individual. In other words, it is locating divine universality within the human being.

In speaking of God's grace, Jesus says that, if we ask, we shall receive and teaches that, in all things, we should do unto others as we would have them do unto us. The transformation of external rules to immanent laws amounts to true humanization.

Rejecting the revenge principle of an eye for an eye and a tooth for a tooth, Jesus says, "But I say unto you, that ye resist not evil: but whosoever shall smite thee on thy right cheek, turn to him the other also" (Matthew 5:39). In place of the principle of hate he teaches love: "Ye have heard that it hath been said, Thou shalt love thy neighbour, and hate thine enemy. But I say unto you, Love your enemies, bless them that curse you, do good to them that hate you, and pray for them which despitefully use you, and persecute you" (Matthew 5:43–44). Behind these teachings is the idea of God as internal law. Law that remains outside without attaining immanence is no more than the hypocrisy of the Pharisees who Jesus condemned. As is written in the New Testament, "the letter of the law kills, but the spirit revives".

I find the idea of the immanence of God and the law consonant with the views of Tolstoy who proclaimed the "Kingdom of God within us".

Gorbachev: I agree that Tolstoy's protests against Orthodox red tape are consonant with Jesus' protests against the Pharisees, and similar red tape resulting from the ossification of Judaism. Though I have never been his disciple, Tolstoy's logic is understandable to me. If my soul is clean, if I do evil to no one, and if my intentions are noble, what difference does it make whether I go to church or pray to God? If I have attained spiritual peace and take joy in doing good for others, then God lives within me. Tolstoy writes in some detail about this in an article entitled "What is religion and what is its essence?", where he says:

Faith is neither hope nor belief; it is a state of mind. It is a person's recognition of his position in the world—a position that obliges him to act in certain ways. A person does not act in accordance with faith because—as the catechism says—he believes in the invisible as in the visible. Nor does he do so in the hope of getting something out of it. He does so solely because, having defined his position in the world, he naturally acts in accordance with that position. (Lev Nikolaevich Tolstoi, *Shukyo-ron Note* [Notes on the Theory of Religion], trans. Hisaichi Hara [Tokyo: Akatuki Shobo, 1949], pp. 35–6)

I have heard that Jesus' injunction to turn the other cheek belongs not so much to Christianity as to Hinduism. Be that as it may, it is a brilliant idea, based on the destruction of deep-rooted stereotypes. It is a distinctive kind of shock therapy, enlightening both sufferer and pain-inflictor.

Ikeda: All religions face the task of preventing their teachings from becoming rules and regulations set down on paper and governing people's spiritual worlds from without. Religion is more than rites and traditions. It is a continual effort of the soul to preserve faith as an inner voice and to protect the secret of the conscience.

As Mahatma Gandhi said, "God did not bear the Cross only 1,900 years ago, but He bears it today, and He dies and is resurrected from day to day. It would be poor comfort to the world if it had to depend upon a historical God who died 2,000 years ago. Do you then preach the God of history, but show Him as He lives today through you" (http://courses.dl.kent.edu/21020/hgandi.htm).

Insofar as Christianity considers Jesus the only son of God—the Messiah—then the immanent law taught by Jesus is capable of ossifying into absolute commandments. This is why we must not conclude that the universal human values included in the Sermon on the Mount are exclusively Christian. This seems to me to be the reason behind Dostoyevsky's ceaseless criticism of the Catholic Church.

Gorbachev: I consider Christ a reformer. His Sermon on the Mount is richer than the Mosaic Law.

Ikeda: I agree. We must inherit and protect the spirit of that reformer, who humanized the teaching of God at the price of his own life.

When Gandhi said we must seek God in the mortal human he took his own view of religion as his point of departure. Considering himself a Hindu, he interpreted religion as something universal that unites all confessions, including Hinduism, and that makes it possible to overcome religious differences. For him, Truth was the basis of all religion. He called God Truth and, emphasizing its universality, said that Truth is

God. According to him, Truth is what the inner voice says, inspiring something hidden in the soul of each person. In other words, by Truth he implies the inner guide orienting a person's actions and way of life. For Gandhi, the essence of faith is striving for Truth, prizing it, and abiding by it. This is the universal religion that is the lasting, inalienable part of human nature.

In connection with universal religion he said: "Indeed religion must permeate all of a person's actions. Only then can it signify faith in the moral law controlling the universe and transcending denominational membership" (*Harijan*, February 10, 1940, p. 445). These words are profoundly similar to the spirit of Buddhism.

Gorbachev: As I understand it, the Sermon on the Mount teaches the importance of being ashamed of criminal thoughts and the controlling of the dark side of the soul. The famous parable asks whether a shepherd with a flock of 100 sheep would not leave the 99 to go in search of one that was lost. Having found it, he would rejoice more over it than over the 99 safe in the fold: "Even so it is not the will of your Father which is in heaven, that one of these little ones should perish" (Matthew 18:14).

Ikeda: The viewpoint reflected in this parable is very important. The 99 sheep represent the world of quantities. The one lost sheep represents the world of qualities, where we deal not with humanity in the abstract but with real individuals.

According to tradition, on his deathbed Shakyamuni said he worried most of all about the fate of a king named Ajatashatru. His disciples asked why. After all, the Buddha should bestow his compassion on all people alike. Shakyamuni replied: "Imagine a family with seven children, one of whom has fallen ill. The parents love all their children equally but are most disturbed over the sick one."

The story was that Devadatta, an apostate disciple of the Buddha, had incited Prince Ajatashatru to kill his own father, King Bimbisara, a follower of Shakyamuni. The patricide then became the ruler of the country. Thereupon, the people stopped believing in the Buddha. Later, the kingdom mutinied and was conquered by foreigners. Ajatashatru himself contracted an incurable, agonizing disease. This is why, worried about the poor king and his people, the spirit of the Buddha could find no peace.

The Buddhist sutras contain many stories about *bodhisattvas*—Buddhists whose souls overflow with philanthropy and compassion. For instance, once in ancient India lived a rich Buddhist named Vimalakirti. A merchant with a family, he took part in politics, helped the needy, and taught them about good. Becoming a lay mentor, he propagated the Buddhist teachings among the simple people, presenting its essence to them in skillful, accessible allegories and parables. Helping them understand their profound inner sense, he brought humanistic Buddhist ideas to life.

Once, when Vimalakirti became ill, Shakyamuni asked his disciples to visit the merchant, but none wished to. It seems that, previously, Vimalakirti had totally defeated some of the most learned disciples in debates on the Law of Life. He had boldly told the priests that they were more concerned about their own authority than about the welfare of the people, and that they preferred to remain isolated from the cares of daily life, shut up in their own world of contemplation. Finally, though unwillingly, the senior disciples Shariputra and Manjushri agreed to go. They found Vimalakirti lying on a bed in an empty room. When asked the cause of his sickness, he replied: "A *bodhisattva* suffers out of sympathy for people... My illness cannot be cured as long as people continue to be sick. When everyone else is free of ailments, I too will get well."

I believe that the full essence of Buddhist humanism is expressed less in verbal sermons than in the acts of adherents of Oriental wisdom. Such acts arise from sympathy and efforts to ease sorrow and lighten the grief of ordinary mortals. These are not, strictly speaking, acts motivated by religion, but they are definitely human.

Gorbachev: As you know, I am neither a theologian nor a specialist on religious problems. My own experience of life guides me in answering your questions. To speak frankly, I have rarely encountered people who approach God in the true, precise sense of the word. I have rarely met people who radiate religious feeling. Probably there are not many. To choose God of one's own volition is an extreme rarity. Most often people turn to God to be in step with their associates—that is, with their brothers in faith. In this connection, I agree with Dostoyevsky, who said the individual human being and the whole human race are subject to a universal and eternal distress about someone to worship. No problem is as uninterrupted and tormenting for free humanity as the need to find someone to bow down to. The object of veneration, however, must be so indisputably recognized as valid that everybody instantaneously agrees in worshipping. Such is human nature.

But the problem has another side, related to the human predisposition to spiritual self-control and self-development and to the understanding of God attained by Lev Tolstoy. We have in fact just been discussing it. I believe that the overwhelming majority of human beings are born with a sense of conscience and of good and that the development of these feelings requires only normal education and a normal family. In communist Soviet Russia, religious believers were persecuted. People were forbidden to read the Bible or discuss their religious feelings. Have you ever asked yourself why, under such circumstances, there were nonetheless many decent, morally sound people? Probably it was because, in the mass, human beings are predisposed to goodness, solidarity, and compassion. As far as moral progress and the possibilities of moral perfection go, I am undoubtedly an optimist.

Ikeda: At the beginning of this part of our discussion you asked whether humanity has the moral and physical power and wisdom to survive new trials. In answer, I should like to share with you my thoughts on the topic of optimism.

I think you will agree that optimism is a fine quality, common to all great individuals, whether they are politicians, social activists, thinkers, philosophers, or artists. True optimism differs from perspectives that open up only under certain material conditions. It is on a different plane. It is created by a person who needs no special conditions to fathom the essence of life. Real optimism is the conviction you talk about. Real optimism is the basic prerequisite enabling a great individual to become great. In true optimism I see the source of the energy of the forces of good connecting all people—all existence—enabling the human being in the darkest moments of life—even in the face of loss of life—to persevere and to believe in the creative possibilities of humanity and its future. This indeed is the source of faith.

Mahayana Buddhism teaches that within each of us is an inviolable essence, as pure and durable as a diamond, called the Buddha nature. When a person is aware of the Buddha within himself and others he is guaranteed true optimism, enabling him to live with inexhaustible hope and to plant it in his associates. The following words of Rabindranath Tagore are pertinent:

Asks the Possible to the Impossible, 'Where is your dwelling place?'
'In the dreams of the Impotent', comes the answer. (Rabindranath Tagore, *Stray Birds* [London: Macmillan, 1917], p. 33)

Gandhi said that his own optimism was founded on faith in the endless abilities of the human being to manifest the spirit of compassion. All religions worthy of their high name ought to be mainstays promoting the cultivation of spiritual values. They must simultaneously teach that, instead of being self-sacrifice, compassion is happiness derived from making others happy.

CHAPTER FOUR

Roots

The Abstraction Trap

Ikeda: We are now witnessing an unheard-of exacerbation of national problems. Intrinsically just and well-founded strivings for national self-determination are often debased into chauvinistic passions and, in some cases, ethnic cleansing. During the past decade or so, national conflicts in formerly socialist nations have grown increasingly violent, notably in the former USSR and in what was Yugoslavia, where nationalist problems remain unsolved. Indeed, now flaring up, now dying down, nationalist passions afflict the entire post-communist expanse.

Even in the West—for instance, in France and Germany—aggravated immigrant and outsider problems spawn lowering clouds of ultranationalism.

In the 1960s, the French philosopher Raymond Aron prophesied that, by the end of the 20th century, ethnic wars would take the place of class battles and the demon of nationalism would replace the devil of class animosity and vengeance. His prophecy is coming true.

Actually, nationalism is nothing new. Ethnic cleansing occurred in Yugoslavia—especially in Croatia—during World War II. In the 1940s, Lenin's internationalism degenerated into Stalinist anti-Semitism. History shows that national—or at an earlier stage, racial or ethnic—consciousness has deeper roots in the human soul than class consciousness. Although it is a product of capitalism and the bourgeois revolutions of the mid-19th century, contemporary European self-awareness has turned out to be an extraordinarily durable and steady formation.

In this connection, the problem of evaluating our understanding of "nation" and "national consciousness" assumes dramatic significance. On the one hand, human beings are not rolling stones; they cannot exist rootless and cut off from the ethnic umbilical cord, ignorant of origins and ancestry. Awareness of ethnic membership is a natural part of the human *I*. On the other hand, the transition from ethnic to national identification frequently leads to chauvinism and the notion of superiority over other nations. More often than not, national exclusivity leads to ethnic wars. For example, the idea of the superiority of the German nation lay at the heart of Hitlerist fascism. Perhaps contemporary civilization should question the concept of the nation state and shift the emphasis to global, instead of merely national, citizenship.

Doctrines of national identity are often imposed from above as unifying stimuli. No idea of a German nation existed before Bismarck's wars of unification. Later, however, Germany unleashed two world wars on the strength of their idea of German nationality.

The concept of the Japanese nation, too, is a product of modern times. Until the Meiji period (1868–1912), the Japanese people considered themselves members of one of hundreds of feudal clans. Formulated during the Edo period (1603–1867), the clan system dates back to more ancient ancestral communities that united people living in a single region and sharing the same traditions.

The population of the Soviet Union, located in the heart of the Eurasian continent, was made up of more than 150 different nationalities living under complex historic and geographic conditions that intensified national and racial mingling and revealed the error of the nation concept more forcefully than is the case in more homogenous societies like that of Japan. Many of the nations of the former Soviet Union trace their origins to an ideology—that is, to the government. For this reason, and because of extreme geographic diversity, the historical roots of the post-Soviet nations are tangled.

The time has come for a new self-identification, broader and safer than the concept of nationality. Perhaps a questioning reappraisal of the idea of the nation would calm hotheads, temper emotions, and save humanity from the fires of new wars.

Gorbachev: Ethnocentrism—attempts to reduce all blood-related problems to ethnic conflicts—is a tremendous danger in our times. It is an illness that has caused many bloody tragedies in the former Soviet Union. That is why Russia must avoid ethnic nationalism. As a counter to it, I propose a civilized understanding of the nation, founded on the historic and cultural unity of peoples and their shared responsibility for the fate of their government, regardless of tribal membership.

Ikeda: Possibly we should simply differentiate protective nationalism of the kind on which Asian and African national-liberation movements were founded from aggressive nationalism like that of the Nazi fascists. We could then concentrate on neutralizing the emergence of aggressive nationalism by cultivating global awareness.

Gorbachev: Yes, of course. And here I call on Berdyaev to be my ally. Instead of "globalism" he spoke in terms of "universalism". But the idea is the same. For me, the important thing is his central idea of shifting from a sense of belonging to a nation to a sense of belonging to the human race.

Ikeda: Berdyaev urged European nations to adopt universalism at the time of World War I. His optimistic belief that they would respond proved unjustified. Although class abstractions did in fact recede, instead of yielding to universalism, nationalism was transformed into an absolute—an idol—demanding inordinate sacrifices. Indeed, nowhere has the poison of an abstract thought so penetrated the human soul as in the case of the nation concept. We must give it another interpretation.

Gorbachev: When they regard abstract concepts as absolutes, the wisest counsel runs off human beings like water off a duck's back. The tragedy of the 20th century was that, as a rule, people heeded counsel only after it was too late and the important chance had been missed.

Today, dialogue about the national issue is gaining momentum in a considerable part of the post-Soviet zone. Increasingly, people are coming to understand that, as our common home, the Soviet Union guaranteed us peace and security. They see that we are connected by a common history and that we must in no case break the economic, cultural, and spiritual connections formed over centuries.

But all of this was said many times before the collapse of the Soviet Union. Even before the signing of the Belovezh Agreement setting up the Commonwealth of Independent States, I told parliament members that the collapse of our multinational society would bring millions of people unhappiness, outweighing all temporary advantages of separation. Most absurd of all, those who instigated and brought about the collapse of the Soviet Union—that is, of the historically formed Russian government—were politicians of the Russian Federation, people who supposedly spoke in the name of Russian interests.

The Ukrainians had never had a government of their own. Therefore, to an extent, their striving to form an independent state is understandable. On the eve of the referendum on Ukrainian statehood, in an interview on Ukrainian television, I warned the population of the republic that trouble would result from separation from Russia. I told them that the Soviet government belonged to the Ukrainians just as much as to the Russians. I said: "We share the same historical course. Such is the reality we have created, for better or worse, successfully or unsuccessfully, over ten centuries. Slavs in general—Russians and Ukrainians—participated like blood brothers in the formulation of this complex and enormous world. We have played the deciding role."

Ikeda: Historic truth was on your side. The influence on Russian culture of literature and traditions born in the area centered on the Ukraine's Kiev and Russia's Novgorod, known to history as Kievan Rus, has been very great. For instance, Kievan versions of sacred texts were in use in Russia until the liturgical reforms of the Moscow patriarch Nikon (1645–76).

Gorbachev: It is very hard to understand what Russian politics and the Russian parliament became independent of. Was it independence from Russian history? From the centuries-old Russian state? From the Russian center? That the Russians gained independence from Russian history! That Moscow became independent of Moscow! Colossal absurdity!

Just half a year before December, 1991, my opponents—all Russian politicians—agreed with me that Russia and the Union needed each other. But, in battling with an abstract so-called "empire", they destroyed a living country.

Ikeda: Abstract concepts have a powerful momentum of their own. Once they are fully charged, an irresistible force keeps them going. Permit me to give an example.

The Russo-Japanese war of 1904–05 is a gloomy part of the history of relations between our two nations. As is now apparent, although nominally the victor, Japan had exhausted all her forces and had reached a limit beyond which further military action was impossible. At this stage, with the mediation of the American president Theodore Roosevelt, the Treaty of Portsmouth was concluded, and Japan was counted the victor.

But Japanese public opinion considered the treaty unfair. Many expressed dissatisfaction that Japan had received very little after having sacrificed a great deal. The government was judged weak, and the public began demanding revenge. This social unrest created the background for the emergence of militarism, the ideological mainstay of which was State Shinto.

Journalists inflamed the passion for revenge that ultimately led to the catastrophe of 1945. They mercilessly exploited incipient Japanese national feelings, inspired chauvinistic ideas, and urged military expansion.

The whole history of the origin of Japanese militarism teaches us to take a cautious view of both the concept of the nation and the mass-communications media, which sometimes play nasty games with national pride. By its very nature, freedom of mass-communications is a two-edged sword. It can serve the interests of the people, but at the same time it can plunge them into an abyss of disaster.

Gorbachev: Russia today demonstrates the verbal madness in which freedom of speech is used as a tool to make fools of the people and to kindle hatred for one's own country and history. My political opponents on the left—the radical democrats—reasoned that we had no homeland, only an "empire".

This is an example of what you call the abstraction trap. Substitute the concept of "empire" for those of the USSR and Russia, and the deed is done. The fates of millions of people were at stake, along with the union of the peoples of Russia—a union centuries in the making—and, ultimately, the fates of individual nations. No one cared.

I would not exaggerate the role of nationalism and nationalistic feelings in the collapse of the Soviet Union. The idea of doing away with the "Soviet Empire" and the Union arose in radical intellectual circles long before it did among the populations of individual republics. It is true that the Baltic nations wanted to restore their lost statehoods. All the other peoples, however, were eager to eliminate centralism and to reform, not abolish, the Union.

Ikeda: Surveys of public opinion at the time showed that, aside from the three Baltic states, the overwhelming majority of republics wanted to retain the Union.

Gorbachev: Comparisons between the Russian and the British empires have been drawn but are easily refuted. In the pure sense, we never had a central government distinct from colonies. Russia belonged to all who believed themselves to be Russians. Russian culture and the contemporary Russian language belonged and belong equally to all the peoples of our nation. In his famous testament, Aleksandr Pushkin, the greatest Russian poet, wrote that his work was a real monument addressed to "all Great Russia" and to every person sharing her language. He added that the Russian language appeals alike to the proud grandchild of the Slavs, to the Finn, to the "now wild Tungus", and to the Kalmyk, "friend of the steppes". The widespread use of the Russian language, however, did not constitute suppression of the ethnic and linguistic diversity of non-Russian peoples.

It would never have occurred to the great English poets and writers contemporary with Pushkin—like Byron—to bequeath their works to the peoples of Equatorial Africa or India. Herein lies the defining difference. For Pushkin, Great Russia meant the solemn concept of the Russian Empire. For Byron, England was only an island.

Of course, the contemporary English are no more a pure nation than we Russians are. Initially Romanized Celts, they have mixed with the Angles and the Saxons—both Germanic tribes. They were later conquered by Normans, who were Gallicized Norwegians. And the descendents of these once very different ethnic groups today call themselves the English.

Though India was counted part of the empire for three centuries, the English were far from mixing with the aborigines, whom they never regarded as their equals. The English established a truly imperial union in which everybody knew perfectly well who governed.

In the Russian Empire, on the other hand, all ethnic groups had the same rights. All nations governed, and the Russian nobility was as ethnically diverse as the whole country. Baltic barons, Tartar princes, and descendents of Georgian tsars all appeared at the Russian imperial court.

It is impossible to transfer stereotyped ideas about empire to Russia and, even less so, to the Soviet Union. Our state expanded in concentric circles following settlement by Russian tribes and was accompanied by tribal and racial merging.

Ikeda: Your statement to the effect that Russia belongs to everyone who considers himself a Russian contains the key to the national problems facing your country. The Russians have gone far towards interpreting Russian nationality on the basis of more than ethnicity and race. I hope that you will go on interpreting "nation" in cultural terms. Russians attribute no great significance to ethnic differences. This probably explains why the Japanese feel comfortable in Russia. Our students at Moscow University and other institutions of higher learning have told me that, in Russia, they never encounter racial discrimination of the kind that is deep-rooted in Western Europe and America.

Gorbachev: Even our Russian nationalists are compelled to admit that, under present circumstances, talk of Russian ethnic purity is nonsense. In incorporating vast stretches of our country, Russians inevitably came into conflict with local populations both in the north and in the south. Our history contains seizures, destruction of refractory tribes, and the shame of the Pale of Settlement for the Jews. But they were not the most important things. The vital point is that, under the Russian Empire and later under the Soviet Union, there evolved a single organic world, where everything—culture, customs, and human destinies—was interlaced. I am not talking about naturally emerging divisions of labor. No matter where they lived and no matter what their national background, everyone in the vast territory of the state felt themselves at home and protected by the law.

The ideologists of dissolution knew perfectly well that tens of millions of people lived outside the boundaries of their own national republics. They were aware that the more than 25 million ethnic Russians living outside the Russian Federation would suffer most from the collapse of the USSR.

Ikeda: Abstractions of concepts—"nation" or "self-determination" as well as "class enemies" and "dictatorship of the proletariat"—have victimized millions of innocent people. The dissolution of the USSR is a striking example.

Gorbachev: Long before the collapse of the Soviet Union and the Belovezh Agreement, I called detractors of the central government and the Soviet Empire neo-Bolsheviks. Intellectual impatience was the source of their revolutionary maximalism and their striving to destroy in a day something that had taken an age to build. It was also the source of their doctrinaire attitude and their alienation from real life and the actual interests of the people. Many of them came to politics from scientific organizations. They had ideas but were very inexperienced.

No one describes the situation better than Berdyaev, our first critic of Bolshevik over-simplification and maximalism:

> Doctrinaire abstract politics is always third-rate. It lacks concrete intuition for life, historical instinct and perspicacity, sensitivity, flexibility, and plasticity. It is like a person with a stiff neck who can see only in one direction and observe only one point. All the complexity of life escapes his view. Vital reactions to life are missing. In politics, abstraction amounts to the facile, irresponsible proclamation of commonplaces unrelated to imminent life problems and to the historic moment. This is why it involves no creative thinking on complicated matters. It is enough to read a few paragraphs from a short catechesis pulled from the pocket. Abstract, maximalist politics always violates life and its organic growth and flowering.

Ikeda: Scientists and scientific workers play—and are going to continue to play—a big role in forming public opinion. But the massive influx of scientists into politics is less a blessing than a curse. Even worse is the advent of semi-scientists and the half-educated. In all revolutions, violence has risen first among leaders who were pseudo-scholars. As was evident among Russian Marxists at the beginning of the 20th century, such leaders make pretensions to knowledge of ultimate truth. They pretend to play the role of the avant-garde mandated to lead the uneducated masses. They pretend to be teachers and educators of the retarded masses. They refuse to wait until the revolutionary mood of the masses rises to the level of their own scientific consciousness. They forcibly inculcate their own abstract truths into the popular mind. During the Bolshevik revolution of 1917–18 they provoked among the people the desire to punish the bourgeoisie.

Slaves to abstract thought and the scientific search for truth, when they revolt, scientists are doomed to a break with real life, which refuses to fit the Procrustean bed of abstract thought. The more they agitate—often artificially—revolutionary moods from above, the greater grows the rift between their world-reconstruction programs and real popular interests and aspirations. Before long, the revolutionary avant-garde grows dissatisfied with its people. The so-called scientific leaders are no longer in a condition to react to the moods of the masses. They are drawn along by the inertia of their abstract programs. Yielding to the whisperings of the devil, they begin to punish the people for disobeying science and the revolution. They start struggling against the counter-revolutionary ideas of the backward masses.

This is why all revolutions entail so much lawlessness, bloodshed, and violence. Recruited from the realm of false science, the revolutionary avant-garde prefers to perish with glory in the name of their ideals and cannot be reconciled to defeat in the face of life.

Gorbachev: All revolutionary extremists insist on destroying the customary order of things. Trotsky gave classical expression to this attitude in his theory of permanent revolution. At the heart of this theory is the idea that equilibrium is in itself evil, no matter how people understand it or what concrete benefits it has brought. Trotsky thought that society must be constantly molting. According to him, one stage of formation flows directly from another. Revolutions of the economy, technology, knowledge, the family, lifestyles, and morality unfold in mutual relation to each other without allowing society to attain equilibrium.

Ikeda: In Asia, Maoism represents the theory of permanent revolution rooted in Marx's call to reform the world. To speak honestly, it was attractive though unrealistic. It promised the impossible and attracted people, especially young people, to the creation of the impossible—that is, of Utopia.

But its conceited, intolerant avant-garde caused enormous tragedy and suffering. To prevent the recurrence of such things, we must restrict Utopian propaganda and make gradualness and continuity with the past paramount. As a rule, people do not willingly break with the past until the new has taken firm root. A break with continuity becomes possible only when the new has prevailed in the natural course of things. This is why people quickly become disenchanted with revolutionary extremism.

In real life, we must stick to the principle that one step forward by a hundred people is more valuable than a hundred steps by one.

Gorbachev: As I have already said, the main idea of our new approach was to oppose doctrinism, oversimplification, and the ideology of uniformity with the philosophy of diversity and a world of multiple values. Of course, I agree that being carried away with abstract ideas and affording them absolute value can be spontaneous and that people sometimes fall into the trap posed by generalities without malicious intent. For instance, at one time, Sakharov proposed that every ethnic group living in the territory of the USSR should form its own independent state and that each block in the foundation of the Soviet pyramid should begin its own independent existence.

Sakharov suggested these things because for him self-determination was an absolute. He proposed that small ethnic groups of several thousands of individuals should have the same rights as big nations like the Germans and the Russians have. His idealism resulted from the mingling of concepts like ethnic group, people, and nation. Unfortunately, as the saying goes, the Russian peasant never crosses himself till it thunders. And it is only recently that we have come to see how dangerous the well-known formula about self-determination is.

I have the greatest respect for the idea of self-determination. But I always ask myself, "At what price?" What is to be done about border integrity? What would happen to Europe and its states if every ethnic group should start wanting its own independent state?

The local ethnic group is in no position to guarantee and firmly retain either security or economic independence. It quickly becomes a pawn in the hands of the powerful. And this means new partitionings, conflicts, and wars.

Ikeda: Inability to combine the principle of self-determination with the principle of territorial integrity accounts for the tragedy of Yugoslavia.

Gorbachev: If we look to life and all its manifestations, the trap of abstraction and the temptations associated with it are puny and can be avoided. But we must stress the cognitive and practical aspects of abstract thought.

As is said, in the beginning was the Word. We became human solely thanks to the Word and to our having mastered the art of abstraction. The ability to distinguish between things and concepts about them stimulated human spiritual development. From the Word evolved time and the ability to tell the present from the future.

Most important of all, owing to concepts like morality, the family, God, the collective, the nation, class, and the state, we learned to correlate our own interests with those of others and to restrain our natural egoism. Christ's Sermon on the Mount puts the moral with brilliant simplicity: "Therefore in all things whatsoever that you would that men should do to you, do you even so to them; for this is the law and the prophets" (Matthew 7:12). The human being is a social and collective creature incapable of existing outside the frame of collective consciousness.

But, as you say, the art of abstraction and ideas generated with its aid can stimulate both great spiritual exploits and a great spiritual fall. This is the tragic factor.

Cherished ideas like homeland, fatherland, and Mother Russia played an enormous role in the dramatic period—November and December, 1941—of the war with fascist Germany. At the time, Stalin and the national leadership realized that the single slogan "The Socialist Fatherland Is in Peril" was insufficiently inspiring to mobilize the army needed to rebuff the enemy. When the life, death, and independence of a nation is at stake, class values and feuds take second place to national pride—in this case, mainly the national pride of the Great Russians, who shouldered the major burden of the war. In those trying times, we spoke of the greatness of the Russian people. We recognized in the Red Army the heirs of the victorious Russian Army and the great Russian military leaders like Aleksandr Nevsky, Suvorov, Ushakov, and Nakhimov. During the war years, we regained our national history.

But, only four years after the end of the Great Patriotic War of 1941–45, Stalin began using these same ideas with opposite aims. Instead of spiritual motivation, his goals were to hoodwink the people and kindle xenophobia and national animosity. Symbolized by the battle with so-called stateless cosmopolitanism, in moral terms the last years of Stalin's life were the most onerous and loathsome of all. They witnessed the start of the most brazen manipulation of Great Russian national pride. The notion that we had always been preeminent in all fields of knowledge was inculcated in the popular mind at this time. We were taught to believe that Russia was a land of giants. Absurd!

Understanding these phenomena requires no special theory. In the first place, during the Great Patriotic War, national pride was equated with national worth. In the second, during the struggle with so-called stateless cosmopolitanism, national feelings were employed for unseemly political aims, thus provoking Russian chauvinism.

Ikeda: Tragically, in the 20th century, humanity was impotent before the spirit of abstraction. Though layers of abstractions give words meaning, they can also isolate them from the actual phenomena they are supposed to signify. Equating words—like nation—with the reality leads to the trap of abstraction.

Words cannot exhaustively express living reality. We must not succumb to the false notion that it is possible to pin down living, moving things with words. At no other time in history has caution toward ficti-tious concepts been as urgent as it is today. In the 20th century, extraordinary faith—sometimes frivolous, blind, or fantastic—led to unheard-of, terrifying tragedies.

Gorbachev: Indeed, we must cure ourselves of the malady of exag-gerating the significance of words and concepts.

This digression has been both interesting and useful, but I should now like to return to our initial topic—the nation problem. Though we may never think of it, we all possess the sense of nationality. That is the way we are made. The human being must—as we Russians say—lean on something. First his support is family, then kin, then finally the ethnic group. A sense of ethnic or national belonging is one of the defense mechanisms of human culture. It is very simple but essential. In critical moments, national identification can become the means of restraining animal individualism. A person who is aware of his nationality awakens readily to a sense of responsibility in critical moments.

Of course, today, defining nationality solely in terms of ethnic group is ridiculous. As I have already said, our most ardent nationalists are compelled to admit that there is no such thing as Russian ethnic purity. Scratch any Russian or Ukrainian and you will find a Mordvin, a Tartar, a Pole, a Turk, or a Finn. The same kind of thing is true all over the world.

Ikeda: Yes, it can be said of the Japanese, too, who, in general, belong to one nation. By the second half of the 7th century, the Japanese had developed an internal government modeled on political and legal systems borrowed from the Asian continent. Until that time, they had maintained close contacts with the inhabitants of the Korean Peninsula. Literary sources bear witness to the absence of even a language barrier between Japan and the Korean kingdom of Paekche.

It was not until the Meiji period (1868–1912) that the Japanese decided to create a new state on a par with the great powers of Europe and America. The leaders began to instill in the public mind State Shinto and devotion to the emperor as political ideology. In the course of these political developments, the artificial idea of the purity of the Japanese nation (Yamato) came into being. The diversity of dialects in the Japanese language, however, testifies against this purity. So different are the dialects that, in spite of universal education in the standard language, people from one part of the nation often do not understand the speech of people from another.

Gorbachev: At the heart of the Russian nation lies, first of all, a past, present and future cultural community. By this I mean a common cultural heritage, common cultural work, and, of course, common cultural aspirations. In this connection, we are closer to the ancient Greeks and Romans with their civic patriotism.

By its nature, nationalism is a perversion of the awareness of nationality. It is a false, degraded form of national self-assertion. It manifests itself most of all in national egoism, exclusivity, and arrogance. It always generates chauvinism and xenophobia. Nationality, however, is as positive a value as the family, the state, religion, and property.

Ikeda: But, just as the individual must be open to instruction, so all nations and countries must be open to education. With such openness it is always possible to find a common language and engage in dialogue to resolve differences or reduce friction. But, as you say, state nationalism and imperial expansion are always possible in exclusivist nations. The closed spirit always includes fanatical elements that hinder dialogue and threaten the use of force to resolve trivial differences of opinion.

Open to the Whole World

Ikeda: In the 1990s, a wall of animosity made killing a part of daily life for the Armenians and Azerbaijanis. On a television program dealing with the tragedy, I heard a despairing old Armenian woman lament: "We lived together on such friendly terms before! Why do we have to kill each other now?" No doubt this is the kind of thing you dreaded when you started Perestroika. As you foresaw, the ill-considered dissolution of the Soviet Union brought unhappiness and disorder to the seceding republics.

The old woman's attitude indicates how surprisingly cosmopolitan the ordinary people can be. I have learned how true this is from conversations with people from all over the world. In his novel *Barefoot*, the renowned Romanian novelist Zaharia Stancu (1902–74) describes how Romanian and Bulgarian peasants were once able to live in neighborly association in a perfectly natural way. But, with the outbreak of the Turko-Bulgarian war, the Romanian peasants were compelled to fight on the side of the Turks. Ingenuous cosmopolitanism bursts forth in the dialogue of the Romanian peasants in the novel: "Fight with the Bulgarians! What have we got against them? We've been friends all along. It's a good thing Ivan and Stoyan are dead. If they were still alive we'd have to fight them hand to hand. How could we stand the shame? Have we got to fight and shoot each other? O God, O God!"

Fighting with their friends is considered shameful. These apparently simple words express universal human nature and the ethos of co-existence, which is the source of cosmopolitanism.

Gorbachev: Personally, I learned my first lessons in cosmopolitan education at home in Stavropol. It was not theory but the fundamental basics of life in the North Caucasus. There people of many nationalities live side by side, sometimes in the same village or settlement. Preserving their own cultures and traditions, they help each other in time of trouble. They visit, find a common language, and work together. Even today, in spite of the current confusion and outbreaks of nationalist passion, they remain true to the laws of good-neighborliness. And that is not easy to do.

Their own historical experiences have led them to understand the simple truth of living in peace and amity. In 1991, the Balkars—one of several peoples living in the region—were given an opportunity to break away from the Kabardinians—another local people—and to form their own mountain republic. Senior Balkars rejected the idea, saying "In the name of friendship and good-neighborliness we will stay with the Kabardinians. We have remained faithful to each other in harder times, why should we break up now?" The Karachay and Cherkess peoples followed the same course. I locate the key to true cosmopolitanism in this model of the North Caucasian life structure—from the individual and particular to those shared things that unite us all as representatives of the human race.

In my opinion, human beings can respect another culture and appreciate its sense and destiny only when they are closely and wholeheartedly bound to their own national culture and are deeply rooted in their own earth. To reach the heights of world culture, we must stand firm on our own local soil.

Ikeda: Very true. Goethe said that a person who knows no foreign languages does not know his own, and that the power of a living native language lies not in eliminating but in acquiring other languages. His remarks on this topic bear witness to the organic connection between the national and the global.

After the opening up of Japan to the outside world in the late 19th

century, foreigners deeply respected the Japanese for energetically main-
taining their traditional culture as represented by Bushido, the way of
the samurai. The depths of its roots in the popular mind enabled the
traditional culture to mediate in the process of advancing toward global,
universal attitudes.

A certain Japanese warrior named Baba Tatsui proudly walked
American streets in samurai dress, winning both surprise and amity
from local people, who treated him as a guest. Before 1867, the
Tokugawa shogunate sent its first diplomatic mission to America to
deliver ratification of a diplomatic and trade agreement. Admiring the
colorful delegation, Walt Whitman wrote in *Leaves of Grass*:

> OVER the Western sea hither from Niphon come,
> Courteous, the swart-cheek'd two-sworded envoys,
> Leaning back in their open barouches, bare-headed, impassive,
> Ride to-day through Manhattan.

In the late 19th century, Professor E. S. Morse, from Harvard
University, was delighted with the good manners of the Japanese
people, especially the children. Even in a troubled period when the
Tokugawa shogunate had just collapsed and power was being restored
to the circle around the Meiji emperor, time was still devoted to education. Morse was surprised to see that good manners can apparently be
inculcated by something other than strictness. He thought Japanese children were educated and learned obedience under heavenly, caring
conditions. Morse's diary contains the following entry:

A foreigner, after remaining a few months in Japan, slowly begins to realize that,
whereas he thought he could teach the Japanese everything, he finds, to his amazement
and chagrin, that those virtues or attributes which, under the name of humanity are
the burden of our moral teaching at home, the Japanese seem to be born with.
Simplicity of dress, neatness of home, cleanliness of surroundings, a love of nature
and of all natural things, a simple and fascinating art, courtesy of manner, considerations for the feelings of others are characteristic, not only of the more favored classes,
but the possession of the poorest among them. (Edward S. Morse, *Japan Day By Day*
[New York: Houghton Mifflin, 1917], p. 44)

Similar statements indicate that the Japanese of those times respected
their national culture and educational traditions. They won admiration
from foreigners by demonstrating universal human nature.

But these high moral traits were gradually overshadowed. In the
boom years following World War II, the Japanese experienced a so-
called economic miracle that earned us the designation of economic

animals. Once, at a meeting with a Japanese prime minister at the Elysée palace, President de Gaulle was unable to hide his opinion on the subject and referred to the Japanese as "transistor merchants". Unfortunately, his remark was well founded. No matter how strong a nation's economy, it is wrong to forget about preserving spiritual traditions.

Gorbachev: To return to Russian matters, I should like to say that probably nowhere is the dialogue between the national and the universal as clearly demonstrated as in the life of Ivan Sergeyevich Turgenev. A Westernized cosmopolitan, as a young man he went to study at the philosophy faculty of Berlin University and never returned to live permanently in Russia. He traveled about Europe and spent the bulk of his remaining life in France. But he could write creatively only when, in the spring, he went back to his family estate, Spasskoe-Lutovinovo, and sat at the desk in his study, from where he could see the park and the silhouette of the family church through the foliage of the trees. His great talent awoke at such times, and Turgenev worked miracles.

He is a paradox and a lesson from 19th-century Russian history. This most cosmopolitan of writers was the first Russian to speak of the Russian peasant soul in his *A Sportsman's Sketches*. Cosmopolitan and Europeanized, he spoke extremely patriotic words about his people and language: "In days of doubt, in days of gloomy thought about the fate of my homeland, you alone are my support and my stay, O great, mighty, upright, and free Russian language. Without you, could I avoid despair at the sight of what is happening at home? But it is impossible to doubt that the people on whom such a language was bestowed is a great people." These words of a Russian patriot were spoken by a student of Goethe and Hegel.

To let you in on a secret, I count Turgenev a kindred soul. Like him, I have a great weakness for the writer and critic Vissarion Grigoryevich Belinsky (1811–48).

Ikeda: For me Turgenev is connected with a very fond memory. In 1981, after visiting the Soviet Union for the third time, I traveled to Bulgaria where I delivered a lecture at Sophia University. Later, during a conversation at the Japanese embassy, the then ambassador recommended that I read Turgenev's *On the Eve*. I followed his advice, and this superb literary protest affected me like a fresh breeze. The pathos of the book consists in its description of the spiritual awakening of Russia, its strivings for freedom in everything—in social activity, feelings, and private life. Its hero, Insarov, a strong-willed, active revolutionary, exerted a great influence on progressive Russian youth of the time and provoked comments throughout society.

It is said that Tsar Aleksandr II was so shocked by the realities described in Turgenev's *A Sportsman's Sketches* that he liberated the serfs.

Gorbachev: I agree that somewhere deep inside all of us is a sense of belonging to the whole human race and that, in the name of the general universal future, we must do everything possible to cultivate concern with the universal and with the entire planet. But how? This is the main question. It is the key to the problem of cosmopolitanism and to overcoming the national enmity that leads to war. How can we make people ashamed of fighting each other?

There are at least two ways of dealing with this age-old controversy. Superficially, the first way is the simplest. It calls for eliminating national sentiments and memories and training people from the outset to recognize their membership in the global community.

We Russians traveled that road to its end during the great experiment of Bolshevik internationalism. For decades, the propaganda machine and the whole education system instilled in the minds of the Soviet people that "Great October constituted our homeland" and that class membership and class solidarity take precedence over everything.

The Soviet person was a spiritual microcosm. In no other land in the world was the spiritual rapprochement between the European and Asian races as close as it was in the USSR. No one concerned himself about whether Chingiz Aitmatov was a Russian or a Kyrgyz. Everyone respected him equally as a great Soviet writer. That is the way things were. And it is impossible to forget and discard such achievements.

Ikeda: The Soviet experiment with educating international feelings has not yet been fairly evaluated. We must remember the influence it had in other countries. In Japan after World War II, when the bans were lifted, leftist views flooded the country. With their simplicity, dynamism, and messianic significance, slogans like "Manifesto of the Communist Party", "The Proletariat Knows No Homeland", "The Proletariat Has Nothing to Lose but Its Chains", and "Workers of all the countries, Unite!" possessed irresistible power to enchant and entrap idealistic young people. By the 1960s, the scales fell from the eyes of the majority of these leftist young people, who rejected Marxist-Leninist ideology. Paradoxically, many conservative Japanese politicians today make no secret of youthful communist leanings.

It may be too soon to evaluate the socialist experiment fairly and objectively. But clearly the vulgar anticommunism and condemnation of

Soviet history as a black hole that prevailed during the late 1980s and early 1990s is already being discredited. Russian communism was no accident. Russian and European history provoked it, and this is why we must take the experience seriously. Even if, as the Polish-born, former US National Security Advisor Zbigniew Brzezinski said in *The Grand Failure: The Birth and Death of Communism in the 20th Century* (New York: Scribner, 1989), the advent of communism was a historical tragedy, we must try to understand why its ideas were as popular as they were.

Still, an objective evaluation of the communist experiment must not overrate Marx and his immoral theory of the dictatorship of the proletariat. Marxist slogans cannot cover up the millions of sacrifices made in their name. We can only wonder how Marx himself would evaluate his theory were he alive today.

Gorbachev: Just when everyone thought the attainment of the goal was near at hand, when the Soviet People as a new historic human community had taken shape, it all fell apart. Surfacing ethnocentrism and national history engulfed everything. Why did the basis of communist, Bolshevik internationalism turn out to be so shaky?

There is ample reason to presume that communist cosmopolitanism could not triumph for the simple reason that it was based on Utopian thinking. As we have already said, national feelings, like the sense of property, are deep-rooted. We can say unhesitatingly that a person who has not been a citizen of his own country cannot become a global citizen.

As early as World War I, Nicolai Berdyaev warned that cosmopolitanism and the withering away of nations are unrealizable because they are Utopian. He wrote:

> The human being enters humanity through national individuality, as a national, not an abstract person—as a Russian, a Frenchman, a German, or an Englishman. The human being cannot jump across a whole echelon of being. To do so would impoverish and deplete him. We can hope for the brotherhood and uniting of the Russians, the French, the English, the Germans and all the peoples of the Earth; but we cannot hope that all expressions of national countenances—of national spiritual countenances—and culture will disappear from the face of the Earth.

We cannot want the Russians to forget they are Russians, the Kazaks to forget they are Kazaks, or the Georgians to forget they are Georgians. This is where the communist experiment erred. As our 70-year experiment showed, attempts to uproot national and historic memory of everything preceding the socialist revolution produced the wrong effects. Attempting to obliterate everything positive in pre-revolutionary Russian history and total criticism of the autocracy have generated the current idolization of Nicholas II, of his conservative prime minister Stolypin, and of the pre-revolutionary Russian economy. Today, everyone has forgotten the wretched way the pre-revolutionary peasants lived in thatched mud huts, with one pair of shoes for five children, and at the mercy of horrible famine years that took millions of lives.

An analogous distortion occurred in national politics. Attempts to eliminate as fast as possible all national memory and to replace centuries-old ceremonies, traditions, and even religious holidays with new revolutionary holidays gave birth to what might be called a suppressed national awareness, which survived like a landmine beneath proletarian Soviet internationalism. When the official ideology and the fears associated with it weakened, the mine blew up. In place of a feeling of unity and the communality of all peoples on earth, concealed irrational instincts awakened wearing a bestial nationalistic grimace.

Ikeda: The concept of Utopia is dangerous because it grows from exterior, artificially devised interests and operates on artificially devised spiritual needs. Although the human soul has no need of uniformity or general similarities, Utopia calls for the removal of all differences in social life.

Tragically, people who come to power on a wave of exterior incentives and moods can easily use their power resources to split the soul and, with the aid of devised exterior needs, drive out profound interior needs. Ideas and words selected to reinforce exterior convictions spawn blackjacks and prison camps. To prevent this, human beings must return to their interior, natural needs.

Living and acting according to internal convictions is of maximum importance. Without internal stimuli and convictions housed in the depth of the soul, neither the individual personality nor society as a whole can be truly reformed. I am referring not only to the communist ideology, but also to various liberal principles of contemporary democracy in Europe and America. Islamic society rejects these principles because, I suppose, it has no internal incentives for accepting them and instinctively senses that they are being forcibly imposed. In the 21st century we cannot survive without moral support and internal incentives.

Gorbachev: To be totally honest, we must admit that cornered national feelings were not the only hindrance to the formation of a sense of humanity-wide union among the Soviet peoples. Under Iron Curtain conditions, it was impossible to feel that we belonged to the whole world. The Marxist model of educating citizens of the world and overcoming exclusivity and narrowness had nothing in common with Soviet practices of political isolation and closed borders. The French thinker Charles Fourier (1772–1837), who had a strong influence on Marx, advocated the formation of communities—phalanxes in his terminology—whose members, especially the young ones, were supposed to make periodic trips around the world and live for long periods in other countries, associating with their contemporaries.

And with us? Until very recently, more than 90 percent of the population of the USSR had never in their lives crossed the border. Making contact with any of the rare Western visitors incurred the suspicion of the KGB. Sale of Western journalism was banned. And, instead of Glasnost, a single ideology had a monopoly and dissidence was suppressed. We never found a solution to the problem within the framework of the communist experiment.

World Citizenship

Ikeda: Education is the key to awakening and reinforcing good beginnings and to forming a philosophy of peaceful coexistence. My suggestion that the United Nations declare a Decade of Education for World Citizens embodied fundamental concepts like ecology, development, peace, and human rights, and urged the pooling of humanity's intelligence in the name of cultivating citizens of the world. Known as the conscience of America, the late Norman Cousins—with whom I published a book entitled *Dialogue Between Citizens of the World*—had the following to say about education in his *Human Options*:

> The great failure of education—not just in the United States but throughout most of the world—is that it has made people tribe-conscious rather than species-conscious. It has put limited identification ahead of ultimate identification. It has attached value to the things man does but not to what man is. Man's institutions are celebrated but not man himself. Man's power is heralded but the preciousness of life is unsung. There are national anthems but no anthems for humanity. (Norman Cousins, *Human Options* [New York: Berkley Books, 1983], p. 27)

I am in complete agreement. The basic causes of many contemporary international disagreements can be traced to the inability of education to overcome its "narrow seclusion"—its sense of membership in a country or nation—and cross over to the position of the "ultimate unity" of all peoples and nations. Having experienced the consequences of compulsory religious education preceding and during World War II, I fully understand the need to cultivate a sense of belonging to humanity as a whole. Almost by way of atoning for that education, I founded the Soka kindergartens, elementary, junior and senior high schools and

Soka University, the motto of which is "Be the fortress for the peace of humankind". I have wholeheartedly striven to make education assist human beings in manifesting their abilities and to inspire individuals to make contributions to the evolution of an international community.

Pedagogic modes constitute a major difficulty. Teachers must never condescend. All kinds of education—scholastic or social—must be built not on compulsion but on voluntary principles. In other words, education must arise from internal needs.

My own teacher and mentor Josei Toda possessed great pedagogic talents and employed unique teaching methods. For instance, at the opening of his mathematics courses, he customarily asked students if any of them wanted a dog. A forest of hands would go up in the classroom. Looking around the room, he would say, "Now, who shall we give the dog to?" Then he would chalk on the blackboard a big Japanese character for *dog* and ask, "What's that?" When all the children replied that it was *dog*, he would say, "All right, anybody who wants it can have it." After a moment's puzzlement, a child would object, "But that's only the character for *dog*." Then everybody would laugh. With this kind of graphic technique and free discussion he would explain conventional symbols, imperceptibly guiding the children to an understanding of numbers and signs as the foundation of mathematics and accustoming them to abstract thought.

Gorbachev: The theme of globalism is very consonant with Russian philosophy. Probably more than anyone else anywhere, Russian thinkers of the late 19th and early 20th centuries stressed the need "to look after humanity as a whole, as a great collective or social organism, the living members of which are various nations" (Berdyaev).

It is not necessary to agree with Russian messianism or with the idea of Russia as the third Rome. A great deal of this idea is far-fetched. But we must see that universalism and globalism are characteristic features of Russian thought. Russians have always dreamed of sacrificing themselves on the altar of the happiness of other people, thereby saving the world. It is probably no accident that communist messianism sank deep roots precisely in Russia. Though poverty-stricken themselves, Soviet Russians uncomplainingly and, at the outset, enthusiastically helped the national-liberation movements of the peoples of Asia, Africa, Cuba, and other regions. In doing this they were fulfilling what they considered their international duty.

All serious Russian thinkers of the 19th century—Westernizers and Slavophiles alike—talked of the same things: that is, of Russia's global, humanity-wide, universal destiny and the need for Russia to teach humanity something. In his celebrated lecture on Pushkin, Dostoyevsky said: "for the Russian wanderer to find contentment, the whole world must be happy. He will be reconciled at no cheaper rate."

Ikeda: Russian culture, including idealistic philosophy, adheres to the idea of the unity of humanity. That is primarily why we Japanese feel close to it. Interestingly, the idea of Russian-ness has never been narrowly national. It has always encouraged service to humanity and the rejection of ethnic and national considerations in the name of the salvation and prosperity of the universal. I feel an affinity with the Russian philosopher Vladimir Solovyov (1853–1900), who had the courage to oppose so-called patriotic duty and attempts to link the national Russian idea with the liberation of the Serbs and Bulgars. As a counterweight to the national interpretation of the Russian idea, he proposed the universal and religious–spiritual interpretation of the historical Russian mission. He wrote: "The Russian people are Christian and, consequently, to know the true Russian idea, we must not ask ourselves what Russia will do through and for herself, but what she must do in the name of the Christian principle, which she recognizes, and for the good of the whole Christian world, of which she considers herself a part." I believe that when he said "Christian" Solovyov had all humanity in mind.

Cosmopolitan Russian philosophy is close to Buddhism. We, too, believe that delving profoundly into our own histories brings us ultimately to an understanding of the miracle and precious nature of human existence and to recognition of our universal *I*.

Visiting the United States in January 1993, not long after tragic riots among black people in California, I wrote the following verses in the hope of providing moral support to SGI members in Los Angeles who were striving to surmount the wall of racial discrimination:

> The search for roots
> shatters society into thousands of
> fragments,
> causing alienation of neighbors.
> But, plumb further to the depths of life.
> Let the thorough search for your own
> lead you to seek the fundamental roots
> of Humanity.
> Then, at the core of your own mind,
> you are sure to find
> the splendid expanse of the land of
> the Bodhisattvas from the Earth,

[merciful Buddhists engaging real life]
the true home-realm of humanity.
Here are no boundaries
no differences of race or sex.
Only Humanity!
The land of true proof
and ultimate roots where all are
brothers and sisters.
Knowing this means
emerging from the Earth like the Bodhisattvas of
the Lotus Sutra.

In these lines I tried to point out the way to discover the limitless universal *I* within every individual. Buddhist philosophy shows the way, and I abide by it in all aspects of life.

Gorbachev: True universality cannot come to light without the support of individual originality. A person who knows his own history can find undeniable universality and elements common to all humanity within it. Russia is a good example. Anyone who delves deep into Russian national history discovers that its essence is first of all striving for universality and transcending tribal and ethnic isolation. In Russia, only a savage, a militant ignoramus can be a confirmed racist. The whole history of the Russian nation is a chain of transformations in the name of amalgamation with other ethnic groups, a chain of self-abnegations, associations, and borrowings. The Russian people are characterized not by self-sufficiency and xenophobia, but by a striking ability to unite with others. As soon as we realize that our Russian-ness depends on Russian culture, language, and shared history and fate, we can make a breakthrough toward universalism and globalism. Russia herself and her culture are examples of the human commonality, of universality, and of a special political microcosm.

In these conditions, much depends, first of all, on whether we can successfully cultivate popular understanding of and respect for our own history. This is not so much a problem of pedagogics and education as of concrete politics. Essentially, the fate of the present Russian Federation depends—as the fate of the Soviet Union depended—on the ability of the population to adopt a realistic viewpoint and to avoid Utopian notions about the Russian nation.

I am greatly disturbed to see that, whereas ethnocentrism has suffered defeat in the majority of the former Soviet republics, it is rearing its head in the Russian Federation. Some people still support an ethnic Russia and the conversion of the federation into a national

Russian state. I am not exaggerating. Some rightists and leftists, too, assure us that it is necessary to form a national ethnic Russia within the federation so that, for the first time in many centuries, Russia can become a nation state in the true meaning of the word.

Here is the way a writer for the newspaper *Den'* [Day] whipped up passions for the cause:

> The population of Russia is 86 percent ethnic Russians plus a few inhabitants from the countries of the so-called near-abroad. Only 8 percent from national minorities live within the confines of their national territories. By all world standards, we are a mono-national country. There are more Russians in Russia than French in France, Spanish in Spain, or English in England. Why do these countries proclaim themselves unitary, national states while we still consider ourselves a multinational country? The Ukrainians, Latvians, Estonians, and Georgians all declared their new states national and unitary with much smaller percentages of indigenous populations, and the whole world applauded. (No. 32, 1993)

You can see that, under post-Soviet conditions, the diffusion of knowledge about and the cultivation of respect for our national history are our main weapons against nationalism. From its origins, Russia has taken shape as a multinational country. Only an illiterate would liken the processes taking place in the Russian Federation with those taking place in, for example, Estonia. The Russian Federation is only the core—a big one—of the old Soviet Union and of the Russian Empire. That is why it has no choice but to follow the path of unity of peoples that Russia followed for many centuries.

We never had a purely ethnic center because, from the outset, Russia evolved as a multinational union of peoples. The issue is not percentages of ethnic Russians and non-Russians. The point is that all of our non-Russians live on their own land—the Bashkirs in Bashkiria, and the Buryats, Altai, and Adygeans on their own lands. Consequently, for them, the Russian land and state are not just for the Russians but are for them too. This is why we must come to grips with the multinational nature of Russia. No doubt, in the years to come, cultivating a sense of mutual responsibility among nations will be an important part of teaching a sense of universalism and global citizenship. I sometimes think that ultra-nationalism evolves from spiritual weakness and from efforts to forget or shirk responsibility for others.

Ikeda: Not everyone in Russia supports your interpretation of the Russian nation and the meaning of Russian history. I am certain, however, that very soon everyone will see the correctness of your position. Ethnic nationalism is doomed to fail in Russia because, as you explain precisely, it contradicts the whole idea of Russian history and the Russian mentality.

Tolstoy's philosophy of nonviolence is very close in spirit to the nonviolence of Gandhi. Primarily, Gandhi's nonviolence reflects the power of the spirit.

In this connection, I should like to relate a story about Shakyamuni Buddha. Pasenadi, king of a powerful Indian kingdom and contemporary of Shakyamuni, was a Buddhist believer from his youth and revered the Buddha as his teacher. In his later years, Pasenadi came to Shakyamuni to share with him some deeply disturbing thoughts. As the ruler of a great state, he was called upon to assume the seat of judgment. When he did so, however, although he had armed forces and great power, he was unable to command his audiences' absolute attention. He continued:

> But your students, O Buddha, are ideal listeners. When you explain your teachings to gatherings of hundreds, no one dares even to cough. But no, I remember how once a monk did cough and another monk, poking him with his elbow, said 'Quiet, quiet! Don't speak. Our teacher is now explaining the law.' Upon seeing that, O Buddha, I thought, 'This is a rare thing indeed. To win the obedience of so many people without resorting to arms! What can it mean?' I had never seen obedience like that before. So I cannot refrain from expressing my profound conviction, O Buddha, that you are truly enlightened.

The Buddha is the ruler of the spiritual world. Only the person who has fulfilled the supremely difficult task of self-mastery deserves to be called a real victor and truly enlightened. Nothing can damage the self-possession of such a person. Surpassing armed might, the spirit of the enlightened person radiates an inexhaustible power to influence.

CHAPTER FIVE

A New Civilization

The Collapse of Communist Totalitarianism

Ikeda: Our conversations have further convinced me of the similarity of our humanistic views. In many respects we take the same view of the role of the spiritual principle in human life. We both react negatively to nationalism and racism. But, frankly, I find it hard to understand how your humanism and faith in universal values correlate with your adherence to the Soviet socialist idea. Probably you would have stayed in power if, upon your return from the Crimea in 1991, you had fallen in with the general social mood by turning your back on Soviet socialism and Marxism. Instead of doing that, however, you remained firm in your views and insisted that, after the defeat of the putsch leaders, political conditions would be right for the perfection of socialism. You remained true to it, although, by the end of the 1980s, Soviet socialism had discredited itself completely in the eyes of the whole world.

Gorbachev: In Russia too I am asked about this. As you no doubt know, after my retirement I was attacked from various quarters. Fundamentalist communists blamed me for betraying my party and its ideals. Our liberals—radical democrats—still cannot forgive me for consistently underscoring my devotion to what I believed about socialism.

In the late 1980s and early 1990s, Western liberals foresaw the definitive collapse of Soviet socialist ideology in Russia and Eastern Europe. But it should be noted that their prophecies failed to materialize.

The most striking developments took place in Poland. It is well known that the communists and Marxist-Leninists never—either before or after World War II—had as firm a position in Poland as they had in Bulgaria or even Czechoslovakia. After the war, when the Soviet Army occupied the country, socialism—not mere "socialism" but Stalinist socialism—was forcibly imposed there. For the next 40 years, under the leadership of the omnipotent Church of Rome, the population morally and politically opposed the communist party and its ideology. Paradoxically, thanks to communist power and under conditions of real socialism, Poland became the most Catholic country in the world.

Poland is the only nation in Eastern Europe—in the socialist camp—where Stalinist collectivization proved impossible. For years, the country was in a state of chronic political crisis. The population, especially the working class, politically opposed the power of the Polish Workers' Party with periodic incidents like those of 1956, 1970, and 1976. Finally, there was the general revolt of 1980 and 1981 under the banner of Solidarity.

After all this, the irreversible collapse of socialism and socialist ideology in Poland seemed inevitable. At the end of the 1980s, no one in the world would have dared claim that the heirs of the defeated Polish Workers' Party would ever return to power. But, to general amazement, in 1989, four years after a crushing defeat in the first free Polish elections, the communists scored a major victory. The heirs of the Polish Workers' Party—renamed the Polish Socialist Party—organized a left-oriented bloc and won a majority in the Sejm (parliament). They conquered on a wave of dissatisfaction with shock therapy, sweeping privatization, and social polarization. Only a few years after the transition from socialism to capitalism got started, the right had lost a significant part of its social base.

The Polish masses, who had rejected and struggled against socialism, began feeling nostalgic for genuine socialism and the social guarantees it afforded. Today, in Poland, the role of the communists, most especially that of Wladislaw Gomulka, is being objectively evaluated. And the authority of Wojciech Jaruzelski, the final First Secretary of the Polish Workers' Party and my friend, is increasing.

The triumph of the heirs of the Hungarian Workers' (Communist) Party in general elections in 1994 was even more impressive and convincing. Nostalgia in Hungary is greater than it is Poland. The Hungarians are nostalgic for the human socialism of Janos Kadar, for the flourishing collectives, and for general prosperity.

Ikeda: We often hear how the ardent enthusiasm of the masses for democratization and liberalization in the nations of Eastern Europe has begun lapsing into apathy. Inability to revive economies fast enough and disappointment with real conditions in a liberal society have evoked this reaction. But disillusionment with market reforms is not the same thing as reevaluation of socialism and Marxism. In Poland, for example, after the tempests of "shock therapy", the people who came to power were not the former leaders of the Polish Workers' Party. As far as I know, Polish leftists profess social-democratic values. Unlike the Russian communists of today, they have broken with Marxism-Leninism once and for all. They are not so much leftists as anti-traditionalists. They won elections first of all by doing things like opposing the ban on abortions the Polish Catholic Church had imposed.

In short, in Eastern Europe, exaggerated expectations vested in the possibilities of liberal freedoms and ignorance of the strict laws of contemporary capitalist economy evoked disillusionment with liberal reforms.

To those of us who have grown up in an environment of real capitalism, the triumph of liberalism over so-called real socialism seems relative. The flashy brilliance of real capitalism enchanted the people of former socialist nations without warning them of the chill landscape of market reality. The collapse of collectivist ideology reaffirmed human egoism. The peoples of the communist world were unprepared for the severe trials of the capitalist struggle to survive.

When socialism fell apart, the economic man, deprived of all traces of spirituality—with which even Adam Smith endowed humanity—dominated in the West. Contact between the economic reality of the former socialist nations and the economic reality of the West—with the logic of capital—led only to the elimination of the guarantees that genuine socialism really did offer. Liberals bestowed liberty while depriving the people of the guarantee to sufficiency that they formerly enjoyed. The image of freedom appealed to no one when it came in combination with a vision of the hungry and unemployed in the United States. This combination is the source of the disillusionment with reforms in Eastern Europe, especially in Russia.

Because we are familiar with Russian spirituality and humanism, we Japanese find it hard to understand what your reformers had in mind when they resorted to "shock therapy". Perhaps they failed to see that they were pushing the people back into the arms of socialism.

Gorbachev: Today in Russia and the newly independent former Soviet republics, people are suspending judgment on genuine socialism and the socialist ideal. In the elections of 1994 for the Ukrainian parliament the left (the communists and the socialists) won an absolute majority.

The important thing is not statistics but changes in attitude. The frantic anticommunism of 1991, though characteristically Russian, is now regarded as a sign of bad form and political myopia. In general, the people take a positive view of the real social achievements of the Soviet epoch. More and more they prize the social and economic guarantees they enjoyed in the past but have now lost. The time has come, I repeat, for a more thoughtful approach to Soviet history and to the values prized by many generations of Soviet citizens.

Much of the past has died forever. Still, some things remain to influence the social and political development of our country and perhaps of all humanity in the 21st century.

Ikeda: Some aspects of Marxism and communism must not be esteemed too highly. For instance, to actively religious people, Marx's designation of religion as the opiate of the masses is blasphemous. Militant atheism, an aspect of Marx-Leninism, led to the repudiation of freedom of conscience and bans on outstanding achievements and monuments of religious culture—religious philosophy most of all. It also led to repression of the ministers of the church. In my opinion, the Marxist theory of a violent proletarian revolution and the so-called teaching of the dictatorship of the proletariat are dead and condemnable. These are the ideas that stimulated the terror of the Bolshevik revolution

Japanese intellectuals know there is more to Marx's work than the dictatorship of the proletariat. But we remember that other elements of his communist teachings appear side by side with justification of terrorism. It was Marx who wrote: "Revolutionary terrorism is the only way to preserve, simplify, and concentrate the bloodthirsty agony of an old society and the bloody birth pangs of a new society."

It is impossible to excuse or rehabilitate militant atheism, the justification of revolutionary terrorism, and the rejection of universal human morality in the name of class morality. This is why we must distinguish between concepts of socialism in the broad sense of the word and violent socialism.

Gorbachev: I agree. It is possible to determine accurately what of the old socialist baggage has passed away forever, what civilization has cast aside, and what remains. Stalinist practices have died, as have radical, violent communism and communist totalitarianism. We can say without fear of contradiction that Lenin's *Communist Internationale* outlived itself and has passed away.

By their very natures, the crisis of the communist movement and its actual collapse were inevitable. The crisis was born of internal flaws in the "communist idea", the realization of which led to totalitarian systems first in Russia and then in a series of other countries. The model was unnatural and glaringly contradicted human nature, including that of the worker. It was consequently doomed to defeat sooner or later. We might say that total communism suffered total defeat.

Before he advocated the dictatorship of the proletariat and the violent overthrow of the existing system, the young Karl Marx clearly differentiated between genuine and false socialism. During the civil war that started in 1918, Russia was saddled with what was called the practice of military communism. This was very close to what the young Marx called coarse, vulgar, and despotic communism. In Russia, it took the form of general egalitarianism, decisive rejection of economic stimuli, collectivization, prohibition of private property, historical and cultural nihilism, and the cult of violence—all characteristics of Marx's vulgar communism and egalitarianism.

In the early 1840s, Marx harshly criticized this kind of communism as diametrically opposed to humanism. He felt that thinkers who insisted on dictatorship, the violent destruction of the old order, and the denial of personal property were the cause of all the trouble, and sharply criticized Utopian communists and François Babeuf (1760–97), the ideologue of the dictatorship of the working class.

Marx countered coarse communism with genuine humanism in the form of socialist thought that gave preeminence to the all-round development of the individual, the emancipation of talent, and harmonious relations between humanity and Nature. In opposition to the communist man, Marx proposed the socialist man as described in the works of Fourier and Saint Simon.

Ikeda: The various strains of humanistic philosophy have always attracted me. Like the young Dostoyevsky, I am interested in Fourier, a fervent defender of the right to personal happiness—perhaps because he was French and personally very unhappy. In spite of his unhappiness, however, his teachings are very sunny and permeated with a foretaste of happiness. He even thought that human beings have the right to be carefree.

Gorbachev: Socialist ideas of alternating labor and of overcoming the differentiation between mental and physical work and between the town and the country attracted Marx. From this standpoint, the socialist man develops in all respects and harmoniously. Marx writes about this in the concluding parts of his philosophical-economic papers, where, it is true, in several instances he calls his doctrine communism but with an added, different sense. He counters vulgar communism with his own communism, which he characterizes as genuine humanism. For Marx, humanistic communism is socialism.

Ikeda: Marxist humanism appears first of all in the spiritual motives of Marx's scientific and political activities for the sake of the unfortunate, the restoration of human dignity to the worker, and the elimination of social extremes. Certainly, the Marxist goal of all-round, harmonious development of the individual is humane.

All honest people in the epoch of the Industrial Revolution asked themselves why the proletariat in England, the most industrially advanced of nations, lived in such horrifying poverty. Marx's work started with trying to define the reasons for this situation and attempting to rectify it. Without a sense of morality in its incentives, Marxism would never have so clearly triumphed over scientific rationalism and would not have been greeted by people all over the world with religious fervor.

Marx's economic-philosophical papers (1844) opened the way to the revival and reconstruction of humanism. When he spoke of communism as his ideal, he meant humane communism. He wrote that genuine communism as perfect naturalism is equal to humanism and that perfect humanism is equal to naturalism. Real communism is the genuine resolution of contradictions among human beings and between the human being and nature. It is the genuine resolution of the dispute between existence and essence and between the individual and the ethnic group. It is—and knows it is—the solution to the riddles of history.

The energy of youth is apparent in Marx's words and in their strict construction. It seems to me that, their results aside, the new social-science horizons discovered by the young Marx are broader than might have been expected. Marx's avid striving to understand, test, and capture everything was a general challenge and might be called a deformation of the Faustian ego born in the new Europe. Unlike Faust, Marx was strongly influenced by the unquestioning, optimistic 19th-century view of reason and progress. Hunger for abstraction and the striving to reduce all the wealth of social life and human existence to certain stable relations were fundamental to his thought. His economic determinism was both a great scientific discovery and an obstacle in the path to an understanding of the spiritual riches of human life. Engulfed in the discovery that a human being is the aggregate of his social relations, he failed to see that much in the human spirit and thought cannot be reduced to economic conditions.

For example, the inherently human fear of death and dread of the chasm of nonexistence, from which no one returns, persist now as in the past. The sense of conscience, too—another cosmic mystery—is irreducible to economic interests or relations. There is no intelligible materialistic explanation of the nature of the conscience—that is, the nature of morality.

Marx was extremely weak on human conduct. Probably it was necessary to be weak in everything relating to the soul in order to be strong in sociology and abstract thought. Perhaps the fault is not in Marx's soul but in the godless atheistic age in which he worked, a time when everybody was busy unmasking religion. The cognitive limitations of rationalism and Laplace's mechanical determinism, too, had a negative influence on Marx's world outlook. If Marx's knowledge of the human soul can be compared to the physics of the 18th century, Dostoyevsky's understanding of humanity and human conduct is on the level of quantum mechanics. In *Crime and Punishment*, for instance, he bares the nature of the human conscience, which he locates in the depths of existential being.

Gorbachev: Of course, experience accumulated over the 150 years since the writing of the Communist Manifesto allows us to see much that Karl Marx neither saw nor understood. Undeniably, he was a biased scholar scorched by the first revolutionary fires. On the eve of the revolution of 1848–49, in conditions of exacerbated class struggle and initial independent actions on the part of the proletariat, Karl Marx sided with revolutionary communism.

His manifesto is called "Communist" and contains much of the revolutionary maximalism of the communists of the epoch of the French Revolution. Reading the Manifesto of the Communist Party of Marx and Engels we see that, in many ways, Russian communists immediately after the Revolution acted according to Marx and his book. For example, the military organization of industry and agriculture that Trotsky praised in 1919 is foreseen in the Manifesto of the Communist Party.

Even a genius like Karl Marx was unable to transcend the boundaries of the revolutionary experience of his epoch. That is why, in my opinion, we can say with full assurance that, in Russia, defeat was suffered not by socialism but by radical revolutionary communism of the age of mid-19th-century upheavals. The things defeated were total abolition of private property, violent revolutionary overthrow of the capitalist social structure, revolutionary despotism, and absolute complete equality.

Our tragedy was that the ideas practiced in Russia at the beginning of the 20th century were already history by the end of Karl Marx's life. Significantly, in the last years of his life, Engels called his teaching not "communism", but "scientific socialism" and took an increasingly critical view of the idea and practice of revolutionary violence.

By now it is clear that the idea of communism is absolute and total Utopianism. But much more common sense is to be found in the *Utopia* of Thomas More (1478–1535) than in his admirers, such as the Babouvists of the French Revolution or the missionaries of the communist idea during the Russian civil war.

Essentially, as I see it, the basic idea of communism is absolute, complete equality—economic equality most of all. The notions of the withering away of classes, the elimination of differences between physical and mental labor, the fading away of the market and of goods–money relations are logical consequences of the idea of total— or "full", as Lenin liked to say—equality.

It is an attractive concept. But any normal, sober-thinking person sees that eliminating distinctions in wealth, education, and labor will not be achieved even in a couple of centuries or more. In school, my fellow students and I started entertaining questions and doubts on this topic. Nonetheless, in many things, I continued to believe and act according to my belief. After a difficult course of searching and a break with communist Utopia, I still remain devoted to the socialist ideal and consider it an important component in the philosophy of future society.

Ikeda: You mention sober-thinking people. Buddhism attributes great importance to sober thought. In explaining the true essence of faith, Nichiren Daishonin always started with examples from daily life. He said that what we call faith is nothing unusual. It is the natural movement of the soul, a natural condition like that of a woman who cherishes her husband; a man who lays down his life for his wife; parents who, giving no thought to their own safety, stay by their children; or a child who refuses to leave its mother (*WND*, p.1036).

The trouble starts when people abandon sound thinking, when, in the name of some social science, the husband stops protecting his wife, the parents discard their children, and the child leaves the mother. The Marxist class struggle is not merely a deviation from sound thinking. It is madness.

Chingiz Aitmatov told me the tragic story of the boy Pavlik Morozov, who reputedly reported his father to the authorities for antisocial behavior and was then assassinated for what he had done. His tragic story shows how insanely things can go wrong.

Gorbachev: Yes. When ideology held arbitrary sway in Russia, my grandfather used to say something that put matters in sober perspective. He reminded us that "people always need comfortable shoes".

Primordial Utopian communism pushed its adherents toward violence. It still does. To make everyone equal it is necessary to eliminate extraordinary things, like talent. Communists in the French Revolution—the Babouvists—called for the destruction of talented people in the name of the great idea of equality. They said: "If necessary, let all arts perish as long as true equality remains." In Russia when the leftist communists held sway in 1917, manors with libraries were burned, and museums and churches were looted.

Ikeda: Surprisingly, however, all great Russian thinkers warned about the danger of socialist propaganda on Russian soil. This strikes me as indicative of a great Russian contradiction. No one in the world uncovered the moral flaws of the communist Utopia and the risks and threats associated with it as powerfully and convincingly as the Russians. But nowhere else did so many people become advocates of the messianic idea of changing the world and humanity. When, under the influence of the first revolutionary acts of the proletariat in 1848 Marx adopted the communist position of world change, Aleksandr Herzen became an enemy of socialist progress. He perceived moral detriment in the idea of serving a "brilliant future". At a time when it was being idolized, in *From the Other Shore* (*S togo berega*), he sharply criticized idolized progress, comparing it with the god Moloch—mentioned in the Bible—whose worship entailed child sacrifice. He asked, "If progress is our goal, for whom are we working? Who is this Moloch who, though workers approach him and crowds of the exhausted and condemned cry out to him 'We who are about to die salute you!', only mocks bitterly with promises of improvements after their deaths."

"Can you really," he asked, "doom our contemporaries to be unhappy laborers, knee-deep in mud, pulling a barge with a flag bearing a secret rune and the inscription 'Progress'?" It is scarcely surprising that Herzen displayed a strong antipathy for Marxism.

Gorbachev: Actually, Herzen was more a populist—a *narodnik*—than a socialist. He rejected oversimplified Marxist doctrine and was therefore closer than Marx in heart and mind to the lives and passions of the people. Like all Russian philosophers, he was the enemy of violence and radical changes in human nature. He can in no sense be considered the forerunner of Lenin and Bolshevism.

Defeated together with communism was the idea of the complete restructuring and reorienting of history. Interestingly, it was Gracchus Babeuf, the late-18th-century communist, who coined the phrase "new world order". Revolutionary communists always made gestures on a universal scale. They wanted to do more than merely impose their principles: they wanted to impose them on humankind as a whole. In all times and places, messianism—and especially revolutionary communist messianism—leads to the suppression of the individual, to despotism, and to leader worship. At the beginning of Perestroika, we turned away from class morality and from the core idea of revolutionary Marxism. This was in itself a spiritual and political revolution.

I think no one in the whole history of humanity will ever be able to convince the masses to accept total permissiveness and to deny the existence of good and evil.

Now that I have tried to explain what heritage we rejected, it is easier to understand how I perceive socialism and what sense I attach to the concept of the socialistic idea or ideal. I am speaking, of course, of socialism as genuine humanism and of practical politics based on the idea that all human beings are equal, that each is entitled to be happy, that each has a unique life in which to experience the joys of human nature.

Socialism as Genuine Humanism

Ikeda: In 1968, the year of the Prague Spring, people in Japan eagerly discussed so-called "socialism with a human face". About 30 years ago, I initiated discussions of human socialism. In communications with them, I urged the Japanese political party Komeito, which I support, to energize not capitalist logic but humane principles that take the interests of the people into account. Making humanism our goal means giving preeminence to humankind, never as a means, but always as an end in itself.

Is this the sense in which you speak of the socialist idea? May I interpret what you have said as a summons to shift from orthodox Marxism-Leninism to social democracy? The logic of triumphing over revolutionary communism closely resembles the path European social democracy has pursued over the past century. Does this mean that you today occupy the social-democratic position and are a European social democrat?

Gorbachev: Our plans to reform the Communist Party of the Soviet Union into a modern socialist party were not born of imitation or the desire to please. Perestroika, including restructuring the Communist Party, was the answer to the moral and political situation of the leftist movement in the Soviet Union during the 1980s. Actually, the Soviet Communist Party rejected the idea of the dictatorship of the proletariat at an earlier stage of its development. Even into the Perestroika years, however, our dogmatists continued to insist on the class approach to morality and the superiority of socialism over capitalism. As time went by, the educational level of society and popular critical self-awareness reached the point where it was clear that the one-party system, the Marxist-Leninist monopoly, and the Iron Curtain were blatant anachronisms. The entire logic of development compelled us to move to the social-democrat position and admit the basic values of civic society.

Moreover, the shift away from totalitarian ideology was easier to make in the framework of a leftist ideology preserving devotion to ideals of equality and social justice.

As early as the twenty-eighth general assembly of the Communist Party, in 1990, a policy for social-democratization was advanced; solidarity on the basic political values of contemporary civilization was reached; and true democracy with free elections, a multiparty system, and affirmation of human rights was confirmed. We discussed the revival of true sovereignty of the people and, at the same time, formulated the task of transition to a multi-structural market economy with diverse forms of ownership.

The need to reinforce the source of power evoked a transition in the direction of true popular sovereignty. This is why our efforts to do away with the monopoly of the Communist Party and organize free elections on a multi-party basis presupposed the social-democratization of the Party. We followed the path followed at the time by the majority of the ruling communist parties in Eastern Europe, especially in Poland, Hungary, and Bulgaria.

In a sense, the transition was easier for us than for some others like Poland. The Bolsheviks were actually a breakaway faction of the Russian Social Democratic Party, who under the name Mensheviks exerted a strong influence on the pre-revolutionary labor movement.

During World War I, the leaders of the Russian social-democrats—especially Georgy Valentinovich Plekhanov—adopted what was called the defensist posture by supporting the Allies against Germany. This attempt to unite socialist ideas with patriotism characterized the Russian Social Democrats.

The socialists stood for social justice and for the right of each individual to social guarantees and suitable living conditions. They made no pretensions to world dominance or the total re-creation of the nature of humanity and the world. They consistently advocated evolutionary development.

If you examine the history of socialist thought or read either the Russian socialist Herzen or the Frenchman Fourier, you will see that freedom of choice was most sacred to them all. For the socialists, it was always important for people to collectivize voluntarily. The communists, on the other hand, forced a standardized version of happiness on the people. In contrast to them, socialists try to cultivate social harmony and solidarity on the basis of already existing, not of projected future, human passions and spiritual impulses. In this connection they are closer to Christianity than the communist-levelers.

The remarkable recent leftward movement of the Roman Catholic

Church under the papacy of John Paul II is worth noting. In his encyclicals he consistently calls attention to the problems of the working classes and the oppressed, and sharply criticizes the predatory nature of capitalism. In conversations with me, he emphasized the importance of the social idea and sees salvation from revolutionary cataclysms in the creation of a system of social guarantees.

Ikeda: I understand the position of the pope. All religions worthy of the name are founded on a sense of compassion and sympathy for the unfortunate and downtrodden. Socialist ideals such as equality and justice closely relate to the fundamental values of genuine religions. Only religion generates the spirit of compassion that reflects in subsequent human actions. Socialism builds a society in which the human being is bound to share material blessings according to set rules.

I notice that you point to root differences between socialists and communist-levelers. The great Dostoyevsky brilliantly exposed the true—should I say destructive—character of the communist-leveler and located the essence not in a system or organization but in atheism. The Utopianism of leveling-communism demonstrated the arrogance of the contemporary, conceited human notion that knowledge and skill alone can really create an ideal society. With his rare prophetic gifts, Dostoyevsky understood that Marx actually resembled Prometheus, whom his doctoral dissertation praised for defying the gods.

In *The Possessed*, Dostoyevsky described the lamentable fate of young revolutionaries stricken with this diabolic delusion. In *The Brothers Karamazov*, he expressed the same ideas more incisively: "For socialism is not merely the labour question, it is before all things the atheistic question, the question of the form taken by atheism to-day, the question of the tower of Babel built without God, not to mount to heaven from earth but to set up heaven on earth."

Dostoyevsky's predictions were substantiated in the process of post-revolutionary changes to the extent that he came to be called the prophet of the Russian Revolution. As a consequence of its atheistic philosophy, Marxism undertook to replace religion in a godless epoch.

Gorbachev: You correctly underscore the contradictory effects of Marx's Communist Manifesto on the revolutionarily inclined proletariat. On the one hand, it excites the conscience to moral protest by exposing the vices of capitalism. On the other, it deliberately incites hatred and openly calls for destruction and violence. Surprisingly, the Manifesto had the same inciting effect on the working classes not only in the 19th century, but also in the 20th century, when education levels had risen sharply.

Carlo Rosselli, the Italian antifascist and founder of liberal socialism who was assassinated by the Fascists in 1937, wrote that Marxism triumphed not because of its important contributions to knowledge of the capitalist world but because of the firmness with which it convinced its warriors of the rationality of their belief and because of its reliance on precision and practicality, highly fashionable at the time.

Marx's Manifesto is one of the most powerful pamphlets in history. Rereading it reveals the sources of its enormous success. It is hard for anyone to contradict—and impossible for the simple mind falling under its influence for the first time. No other libertarian or man of action has ever been able to arouse such indignation and awaken such fantastic devotion as these famous twenty pages. Its dialectic convinces. And once you are under its sway, it shakes your reason with maxims worthy of a vengeful deity. It is a romantic dream under the guise of sound reasoning.

Though a socialist, Carlo Rosselli was the foe of Marxism and of communist revolution. The socialist heirs of the Second Internationale put greater hopes in collectivist sentiments and the advantages of coop- eration and mutual-aid labor funds. But they never encroached on ownership, traditions of private family life, or market relations.

As Russians like to say, all of today's social democrats popped out of the sleeves of people like Eduard Bernstein (1850–1932) and Karl Johann Kautsky (1854–1938) and therefore grew out of the Marxist tradition.

But I think that, in spirit and in the world view, current social democ- rats are closer to social Utopians than to the thinkers from whom Karl Marx borrowed the concept of the socialist man. Paradoxically, the thinkers Marx called social Utopians turned out to be better prophets than he was. Advocates of the gradual evolutionary reformation of social life and of social guarantees, Saint-Simon and Fourier still and will remain relevant in the 21st century. The ideas of the consumer, marketing, and industrial cooperation developed by social Utopians have been put into practice in all the developed countries of the West, especially in Scandinavia. But no one has been able to realize Marx's dream of turning a national economy into one big, director-dominated factory. Even in Stalinist Russia, peasant family plots produced a large part of the nation's foodstuffs. At the end of his life, Lenin himself began reexamining the role of cooperation within the framework of future civilization.

Lenin's ideas about cooperation, reflected in his theoretic testament, stimulated me to correct my own convictions. After reexamining his whole socialist viewpoint, Lenin decided to bet on the kind of cooperation the dogmatists had rejected. This being the case, surely, knowing the lessons of seventy years' experience with communist experimentation, we too have the right to our own truths and conclusions.

Socialism has a great future as a concept of social guarantees obliging society to care for all its members and to provide them with conditions worthy of humanity. Government may someday retreat from the industrial sphere, but it will never leave the social sphere. Our experience with the development of humanity in the 20th century and especially in Western Europe after Word War II bears witness to the undeviating role of government in the distribution of national wealth and in alleviating social contrasts like the rich–poor gap. Stability is unattainable in a society in which a paltry minority of the rich confronts a poor majority.

Personal property and the market economy are fundamental values of human civilization. But the highest value of all is individual character. For the sake of the individual, an organic combination of liberal values defending the freedom of the private producer with social values defending basic moral and spiritual equality is inevitable. I am not talking about a hodgepodge of ideologies, each struggling for a place in the sun. I mean selecting and finding a way to unite values that both stimulate spiritual and economic development and reinforce personal liberty and the value of every human life.

Ikeda: The bankruptcy of the planned, centralized economy does not entitle the market to assume the arbitrary attitude it adopted in the 19th century. Acceptance of the challenge to socialism, or some of its elements, is what made the triumph of liberalism and the market economy possible.

To one extent or another, even liberal nations with market economies manifest elements of the mixed economy and of social security. In the United States, as the Democrats or Republicans come into power, the political pendulum swings now in the direction of liberalism and now in the direction of official intervention in economic life. The historian Arthur Schlesinger likes to quote Franklin D. Roosevelt to the effect that progress is not measured by the increased wealth of the haves but by the success of our efforts to provide for the have-nots. This is what democratic capitalism means.

One of the major problems confronting the 21st century is establishing equilibrium between the two sides of the contradiction—that is, creating a protected society while promoting entrepreneurial activity. I believe that your choice of social democracy was motivated by striving to arrive at this kind of equilibrium.

Gorbachev: Interestingly, in his later years, having abandoned *Das Kapital* and moved away from politics, Marx too began thinking of the viability of society and to pay attention not to conflict and class struggle, but to harmony and those things that bind human beings together. Although, unfortunately, his new view on society remained undeveloped, it was another small bridge in the transition to social democracy.

Ikeda: Late Marx is indeed an enigma. For instance, in the last phase of his scientific work, in his letters to the Russian revolutionary Vera Zasulich, he formulated a paradigm of social science that was deeper than *Das Kapital*. He adopted a new approach to the definition of the essence and content of social progress. Whereas earlier he had viewed history and social life from the stance of overcoming exploitation, in his letters to Zasulich he proposes to evaluate societies from the viewpoints of their viability and of the eternal struggle between constructive and destructive forces.

Marx's new, undeveloped approach touches on genuinely fundamental problems of human history. Not every regression is followed by progress. We cannot count on extremes always coming together. Unfortunately, the danger of destroying life and the human race exists at every phase of development. Absolute, irremediable regression is a possibility.

Today, we cannot strengthen the viability of society and achieve progress without securing a full life for every individual. The problem boils down to ensuring harmony between the development of personal rights and freedoms and reinforcing the fundamental basis of life.

My own mentor said that the personal happiness of the individual and the well-being of society are inseparable: "Today the object of discussion is society, but we observe that everywhere the individual is being isolated from society. Is not dealing with the incompatibility between social well-being and personal happiness and well-being the age-old task of politics? In a fully prosperous, generally happy society, each individual human being, too, must be happy." The person wishing to serve the name of genuine politics must shoulder the burden of ensuring individual as well as general happiness.

Gorbachev: At the twenty-eighth congress of the Soviet Communist Party, we announced our intention of connecting socialism not with dogmas, but with humanized living conditions and individual well-being, rights, and liberties. We related socialism to genuine humanism in the attainment of these goals. The transition to the social-democratic position was discussed in a projected party program published during the second half of July, 1991.

During the last July plenary session in 1991, I was accused of attempting to convert the Communist Party of the Soviet Union into a social-democratic party. I replied:

> The opposition between the Communist Party of the Soviet Union and today's social-democratic movement is based on logical differences dating to the Revolution and civil war, when the Communists and the Social Democrats were on opposite sides of the barricades. The upheavals of the past are the concern of historians. It is now completely evident that the criteria for the opposition of those times have lost their former significance. We have changed; so has social democracy. The course of history has solved many of the problems that once split the labor and democratic movement and advocates of socialism. People today who are frightened by social-democratic trends are simply closing their eyes to the real enemy: antisocialist, national–chauvinistic tendencies.

There was nothing opportunistic in my transition from the communist to the social-democratic position. As a man of leftist convictions for protecting social justice, I simply followed the logic of the changes in social awareness that had occurred in my own country and throughout the world.

The dramatic events that followed the July 1991 plenary session prevented me from fulfilling my plans. The social-democratization of the Communist Party of the Soviet Union did not take place. Owing to the criminal acts of the putsch leaders, the party collapsed. But I do not think the death of the party means that our plans were mistaken.

Ikeda: I consider the politics and views of the putsch leaders to be not so much communist as ideological fanaticism—a pathology of the consciousness—characteristic of the 20th century. Russia had changed. But, isolated within themselves, they neither wanted to take this into account nor admitted the possibility of other approaches to problems that were coming to a head.

This sickness of self-isolation was characteristic of the European mind in the 20th century. In his major work *Revolt of the Masses* (1930), the Spanish writer and philosopher Jose Ortega y Gasset (1883–1955) revealed and described it. (His book was the same kind of turning point in social science that Rousseau's *Contrat Social* was for the 18th century and Marx's *Das Kapital* was for the 19th century.) In it, Ortega y Gasset wrote that, with syndicalism (the revolutionary doctrine by which workers take over the economy and the government) and Fascism—the underside of society—a new kind of man appeared for the first time in Europe. This new man rigidly insists on his own opinions, without explaining the reasons for his political behavior, trying to convince others, or substantiating his ideas. His advent created a new situation in which the spirit of discussion was sapped at the root and the form of general coexistence—the basis of objective criteria in any discussion, including ordinary conversations, scientific arguments, and parliamentary debates—was hated. Tolerating this situation meant denying the basic norms of civilized existence—that is, a return to a state of barbarism.

For Ortega y Gasset, rejection of culture and a return to barbaric behavior meant limiting moral norms to one's own kin—in the 20th century, to one's own clan, party, or race. This is connected primarily with the self-isolation of the human soul and with instincts for rejecting the other and society. These instincts block the path to dialogue and provoke animosity and cruelty. Although no mention is made of Russia or of Russian communism in *Revolt of the Masses*, patently what is said about syndicalism and Fascism pertains to the Bolshevik social-class interpretation of the world.

An understanding of Bolshevik self-isolation as isolation from culture makes it easier to understand the essence of Perestroika. In my opinion, Glasnost was a return from isolation to the dialogue of culture and to new facets of the free and open human being.

Gorbachev: Fortunately, liberalism did not reign long in Russia. Liberal reforms aimed at making some people as rich as possible and others as poor as possible lasted two years. That was enough for them to earn the hatred of the masses.

In all arguments about effecting reforms, I had the advantage over the liberals in that I knew Russia and what the Russian peasantry breathes. My liberal opponents, advocates of rapid, destructive reforms, were guided only by book-learning.

Take, for example, our arguments between 1989 and 1991 about privatization. I insisted—and proved—that Russia and especially the peasantry would not accept transition to pure private land ownership and that the populace would reject unrestricted sale and purchase of land. Enforced privatization of the collective farms would be as great a calamity as collectivization had been in the 1930s. People accused me of being reactionary and behind the times.

Ultimately, no order concerning the sale and purchase of land was realized. It was adamantly opposed in southern Russia, where Cossack traditions of communal land usage persist. Even in the fertile central part of Russia, many peasants regard proposed liberal land reforms with misgivings. They are unwilling to bear the responsibility for their own plots and fear that, under the present exorbitant credit system, they will lose their holdings. Instead of doing away with collective farms, we must change their fundamental nature by changing property relations. The peasants themselves must freely choose management forms.

Priority of Spiritual Values

Ikeda: That the 20th century was characterized by war and violence is, I believe, due to relegating the human being to second place. Priority was given to systems and material things. We failed to look into the human being, and instead sought both happiness and blame in external—not internal—factors.

Gorbachev: The big question is how to stimulate spirituality, moral and spiritual self-perfection, and individual responsibility for nation, government, and people. Idealists, like Nikolai Berdyaev, felt that all evil in Russia arose from Marxism and materialism, from assigning priority to social forms, and from exaggerated attention to the problem of distribution. Believing this, he urged people to turn from the material to the spiritual and to cultivate and develop individual spirituality as the sole creative power of human existence.

Unless spiritual and moral factors are afforded priority, the world will collapse. But the prognoses of the great thinkers who thought that all the evil was attributable to Marxist materialism proved unjustified. What they had dreamed of happened. All fetters hampering the intellectual, spiritual, and religious development of the nation dropped away. As the legal Marxist Pyotr Struve dreamed, the Russian people were liberated from class-oriented international socialism, from worship of all kinds of political and social forms, and from everything exerting a destructive influence on the popular soul and life. But the collapse of the Soviet Union was a sweeping breakdown of economic, cultural, and plain human relations by a single government. It was therefore accompanied by an unprecedented increase in national nihilism.

During the Soviet period, state-enforced atheism turned the Bible—Old and New Testaments—into a forbidden book. Anybody who declared belief in God became an outcast, effectively denied the right to a higher education and a career. Whole generations in Russia were born and died without the least understanding of the fundamental truths of Christianity or Islam. Nonetheless, many of our unreligious people and even our confirmed atheists betrayed no one, sympathized with the troubles of others, and aided the oppressed and downcast. Under the very same condition, the same party discipline, and the same fear of ruining careers and losing party-membership cards, some people remained loyal friends and aided the unfortunate, whereas others were scoundrels who denounced and came to power literally over the corpses of their associates. In connection with learning lessons of good and evil and the secrets of the human soul, Soviet history is more interesting than the history of any flourishing and successfully developed country.

Ikeda: I have always been impressed by the depth of spirit of the Soviet people. Unique examples of human nobility emerged within the framework of the communist system. In general, I get the impression that Soviet society was on a higher level of spiritual and moral development than the current post-communist society. To corroborate this impression, I might cite the inexhaustible depth of the films of Andrei Tarkovsky and the tragic profundity of the novels of Mikhail Bulgakov and Yevgeny Zamyatin. The theatrical director and musical-educator Natalya Sats (1903–93) created an impression of boundless spiritual warmth in me. And I always find your internal luminescence astonishing.

Probably the roots of the spiritual luminosity of the Soviet people can be traced to instinctive opposition to totalitarianism. Paradoxically, in order to live and accommodate themselves to a harsh ideology, they required maturely developed souls and the courage to experience their own tragic history communally.

The important thing is to ensure that the spiritual experience of the Soviet people is perpetuated in human memory. Culture is not a product of art only. It is also an experience of human life, a special unique movement of the human soul. It is difficult to demonstrate what elements of Soviet spirituality grew from tradition and Russian-ness and what from the misfortunes and dramas of life without freedom. Today, the simplistic black-and-white approach to evaluations of contemporary civilization is regarded as anachronistic. No one would risk saying that democratic nations are more successful in moral relations than totalitarian nations. The crisis of contemporary civilization has touched all countries and all political systems without exception.

In 1987, American readers were stunned by the book *The Closing of the American Mind* by the then little-known Allan Bloom. In a tremendously convincing way, the book disclosed the dead-end in which contemporary American civilization found itself. Bloom has a character in the book—a college freshman—enunciate the anxiety gripping the American university by declaring his wholeness as a human being and demanding to be allowed to develop all his potentialities as a whole. His cry comes from the soul of American civilization. Though America, the so-called leader of contemporary democracy, overcame totalitarianism, it ravaged its own spiritual foundations in the process. It must be admitted that America emerged from the Cold War spiritually devastated. As you quite rightly say, in the Cold War there was neither victor nor vanquished. Both sides lost.

Gorbachev: I do not intend to say that religion is useless or that atheism was beneficial to the Soviet Union. By depriving them of the Bible, the Koran, and the Torah, the Soviet state emasculated people spiritually and culturally.

But I am more concerned about the mechanisms for the stimulation and cultivation of conscience, moral self-control, and self-restriction. In these connections, we, living at the beginning of the 21st century, are no wiser and no more experienced than our predecessors.

Ikeda: In spite of their intellectual power, our contemporaries become increasingly impotent to cultivate moral qualities. The people of the past, however, possessed a very high level of self-control. As is well known, the ancient Greeks knew much more than modern people about the nature of the good.

People today seem to believe that happiness depends solely on external factors and is unrelated to internal defects. They are obsessed by external conditions. Limitless means are applied to working out optimal social systems. Gigantic legal, economic, philosophical, and other mechanisms work to soften the contradictions of modern society. As a rule, these attempts produce varying results, some calming, others disillusioning. Directed toward social reforms, such efforts are necessary and useful. I have nothing against them. Nonetheless, as long as internal evil remains unconquered, combating external evil and encouraging good on the basis of outside conditions can never guarantee happiness. Undeniably, it is better to live in a warm, well-built house than to huddle in a drafty hovel. But we must remember that the beauty of the souls of the mother and father, and not the house, creates the warmth of the family hearth. Families can suffer from chilling discord in the most luxurious residences.

Admittedly, people find satisfaction in combating evil everywhere but in their own souls. In concentrating our gaze on external reforms, we disregard human internal moral reserves. To make society as a whole happy, we must bring happiness and goodness to its individual members.

Gorbachev: While still a student assimilating the basics of humanitarian knowledge, I was interested in the influence living conditions exert on the formation of an individual's philosophy and spiritual aspect. Why do children with totally different spiritual and moral attitudes emerge from a single family where material conditions and education system are the same? Does this indicate an innate, God-given predisposition to good or evil? If not, what are the keys that stimulate morality and spirituality?

In Russia, thanks to the worldwide communist experiment that cost unbearable suffering for millions, we have definitively abandoned many illusions. Our own Soviet experiment tried to make scientific truth and knowledge absolutes. We indulged in legal and normative games that were, as we found out, spiritually and morally neutral. Although evil and cruelty are worse among the ignorant, erudition does not illumine the soul.

We now realize that atheism, which encroaches on the soul and on the search for God, is both amoral and inhuman. In proclaiming freedom from God, atheism essentially proclaims freedom from conscience. In this decisive point between materialism and idealism, Dostoyevsky proved right.

We Russians today have a short supply of the truth that gives precedence to the internal over the external. We must try to discover why we paid no attention to Dostoyevsky's prophecies. Perhaps poverty, disorder, and anguish, or maybe the apparent hopelessness of our situation, blinded us. Certainly, external factors have one value for the prosperous and an entirely different one for the poverty-stricken and oppressed. If we do not deal with the problem of external factors, without material prosperity, we will remain trapped in our vicious circle.

Ikeda: We must do everything possible to ensure that the 21st century is devoted to the principle of the sanctity of life. As we have said, Albert Schweitzer considered life itself the paramount value. We must understand how its supreme value can guide us in everyday life. The issues of life and death and the understanding of the ephemeral nature of our existence provide a system of coordinates within which each individual can consider all serious questions.

We must realize that a last day will come. Ideally, each human being should regard every act as final and irremediable. This is very hard to do. Constant awareness of the end of life can become depressing. Nonetheless, somewhere in our subconscious, we must be aware of the finiteness of our existence. As paradoxical as it seems, the consciousness of death enriches life. Would the human being be happier if immortal? Hardly: immortality would make him inhuman by depriving him of the fear of making irreparable mistakes. The human hopes close associates will remember him as worthy of respect. The knowledge of the finite nature of life prevents the spiritually developed person from putting things off and stimulates him to do everything possible to establish himself as an individual right now. To a large extent, understanding the finiteness of existence determines one's interpretation of the meaning of life. It keeps us from postponing good deeds and keeps us constantly aware of our responsibility for our actions.

Buddhism teaches that the force of life itself is eternal, without beginning or end. It manifests itself in passive, sleeplike phases and waking phases—that is, in death and life. Each of us awakes each morning the same person that went to bed the night before. In the same way, after death the same life entity awakens. Life itself is a continuum that makes us always aware of mortality and immortality at a profound level. Human beings are capable of doing good and moral deeds only when they sense within themselves the shifting boundary between death and life. This is why awareness of death generates and illuminates the spiritual life.

The purpose of religion is not merely to spare us suffering. Limiting religion in this way is degrading. Although secular and spiritual functions correspond differently in different belief systems, the true purpose of religion is to reveal the secret of life and death and the nature of the spiritual principle. As is illustrated by Jesus' injunction to render unto Caesar the things that are Caesar's and unto God the things that are God's, Christianity distinguishes between the secular and the spiritual. In Buddhism—especially Mahayana Buddhism—on the other hand, the secular and the spiritual are inseparable.

Gorbachev: Russian peasant life is part of my soul. My personal experience with it has taught me that the ordinary Russian people share a single system of values. For them, the teachings of religion and standards of behavior are a whole. Those who sincerely believed in God did all they could to avoid sin and worried about their reputations. This attitude evolves from the Russian spirit and from Russian Orthodoxy.

In writing about Pushkin, in a favorite passage of mine, Dostoyevsky mentions the ability of the Russians to understand other people. Dostoyevsky put it better than I can when he wrote to the effect that the Russian soul—the Russian genius—more than that of any other people embodies the ideas of universal unity, brotherly love, sober views, forgiveness for hostility, discerning and forgiving dissimilarities, and removing contradictions.

Ikeda: Your country is a cultural colossus, and Dostoyevsky's statement eloquently affirms the profundity of Russian culture. Because all of them are nurtured in universal human nature, true works of art myste-riously compel us to forget social ranks—president, private soldier, specialist, or janitor—and don our genuine humanity. In our world of differences, we require an area where all of us are equally worthy. The great sea of art is such an area; it enriches us and makes us feel at home and free.

Culture and art are like the petals of roses blooming on thorny bushes. Real life has its thorns, but good deeds and compassion make the human being beautiful. Instead of being created by the turbulent surface waves of political and economic affairs, history is the slow, profound ocean current where culture, art, and education play leading roles.

Gorbachev: As you no doubt know, Russian geniuses, especially Tolstoy, had great regard for Buddhism. Today we are in still greater need of Eastern circumspection, calm, and respect for tradition.

October 1993 was a black time for Russia, a time when force was used to bombard the seat of national government. On the eve of each anniversary of those events, I reflect on what happened and for a long time found myself unable to understand why the people remained silent. This was the most shocking thing of all. Why do they remain silent today? Finally the impenetrable became clear to me. The people are not silent. Spiritually they are still very much alive. But they are wise. They see and understand. They are keeping calm. The most important thing now is to prevent the occurrence of catastrophe. Today Russia is held together by the common sense of reasonable businessmen who calmly go about their work.

At the beginning of Perestroika, while preparing a political report for the twenty-seventh conference of the Communist Party, my associates and I were trying to find the safest and least painful way to express our new humanistic world views. As strange as it may seem, Lenin and Marx often came to our aid. For instance, in one of Lenin's works I discovered ideas on the priority of the interests of society as a whole over those of the proletariat. This gave me the key to my own study of correlations between class and general human values. For the first time, I said what I had long thought: the meaning of civilization, progress, and culture exists only in preserving human life, on which everything else depends.

In the fearsome 20th century, many clever and wise things were said about human life and its value and about the greatness of nature and humanity. When I was still secretary general, I received—as was customary—the first copy of a Russian translation of the collected works of the Japanese author and nature artist Roka Tokutomi (1868–1927). I took the little book home and gave it to my wife, Raisa Maksimovna. After she went into raptures over it, I read it too. As a man of peasant background, whose forefathers worked the land for centuries, I was most impressed by Tokutomi's ideas about the unity of the land, the human being, and life. He wrote that we are born on the land. We live on it and are fed by what it produces. When we die, we return to it. Ultimately, he says, the human being can be considered an incarnation of the land. This is why working the land is the most suitable of all occupations. The farmer has selected the very best of all the possible ways of living on earth.

Ikeda: His works—especially *Nature and Life*—were favorite reading for me in my youth. I am pleased that Roka Tokutomi made such a deep impression on you and your wife.

You and I grew up sensing the boundless expanse of life. Since the second half of the 20th century, however, intense environmental destruction has compelled people to exist in a natural world that is steadily being impoverished.

Gorbachev: I am proud that people who devote their lives to saving the natural environment of our planet elected me president of the Green Cross International. I consider my having been awarded the Albert Schweitzer Prize, too, very valuable. During his life as a missionary, Schweitzer tried to resolve the problem we address: laying the groundwork of a new humanism. In *Civilization and Ethics*, he wrote that, on the basis of a new understanding of the good and ethics, morality requires internal incentive to help all forms of life capable of being helped and to refrain from harming any living creature. The moral man never asks whether a life form deserves having efforts made in its name. He never asks whether a life form is cognizant of what is being done for it. For the moral person, life is sacred of itself. Much of this approach to morality and life transcends 20th-century mechanistic interpretations of man the inventor, the conqueror of nature, the crusher of the world and its customary order, and a being free of responsibility for the consequences of his actions.

Actually, only since the middle of the 20th century have human beings faced their own mortality and opened their eyes to the limitations on our abilities to break and remake nature. Only when they began understanding these things did they come to realize that negation of the past does not always mean a step upward. We have come to see that some such negations are followed by oblivion.

Much is being said about the current crisis of human civilization. In my opinion, it is the crisis and ultimate degeneration of the expansionist ideology. There is no longer any meaningful distinction among types and forms of expansionism—for instance, between communistic and scientific expansionism. There is no difference now between striving to subordinate everything to the idea of equality and striving to subordinate everything to science.

Ikeda: Long gone are those happy times when it was possible to believe that reason and science guarantee progress and development. As early as the end of the 19th century, leading minds doubting the very essence of contemporary civilization sounded the warning. Now the threats buried in the depths of European ideology have surfaced.

The French poet-philosopher Paul Valéry devoted much of his attention to the negative consequences of European expansionist ideology. He wrote that dominance by the European spirit means the appearance of extremes in desires, work, capital, productivity, ambition, power, environmental changes, trade, and negotiations. All these extremes constitute the face of Europe. Unfortunately, the expansionist European ideology now reigns in Asia too. Having succeeded in destroying nature, we strive for extremes in everything.

In Valéry's view, the destructive side of the European spirit consists in the growing, insatiable thirst that stimulated the development of contemporary civilization. Now, however, expansionism has run up against a solid wall. Unless we find some way to limit the will and thirst for striving for extremes, our civilization is doomed to disappear.

This situation reminds me of the Eastern allegory of the dread of the twenty-ninth day. The story goes like this: Some leaves of a single lotus plant fell into a pond one day. The next day, the quantity of leaves had doubled, and doubled again, day after day. In thirty days the pond was completely covered with lotus leaves. On the twenty-ninth day, when leaves covered only half the pond, no one thought the whole pond would be covered the very next day. In fact, there really was only one day of grace. With crises in population, resources, and energy, contemporary civilization is at the twenty-ninth day. Possibly, by the thirtieth, nothing at all will remain.

Gorbachev: The situation permits no delay. The present crisis has a special character because we have just recently clearly discerned the possibility of self-destruction. If the conflict with nature is not resolved, humanity faces consequences comparable only with those of nuclear war.

Far from ameliorating it, the techno-genous process actually deepened the conflict. In the past few years, thunderous warnings have rumbled on several occasions in the form of the greenhouse effect, holes in the ozone layer, erosion and depletion of top soil, and pollution of the oceans. But politicians have paid too little attention. They struggle for power and spheres of influence without noticing that the ground under their feet is on fire and may soon fall from under them. It is now obvious that the ecological crisis originates in a crisis of traditional value criteria and controls. It is a crisis of spirit and world-outlook.

Though much of his thought was beyond us, in our student days we read Goethe. As Marxists, we were Hegelians, believing there could be no progress without negation of the past. We thought that the more vigorous the negation and the more active the struggle against hang-overs from the past, the greater the hope of future prosperity. But Goethe waged a passionate argument against Hegel and the illusions of an age of prosperity and endless progress. He advised humanity to obey nature, abide by its law, and never exceed its limits.

Ikeda: Goethe rejected the French Revolution on the strength of his organic sense of life. In this he was wiser than Hegel, who greeted the overthrow of the French monarchy ecstatically. Of course, Goethe was older, more experienced, and therefore more cautious. These factors played a role in his reaction. His concept of gradual progress opposed revolutionary violence. In Russia, Pasternak, Chaliapin and Bunin inherited Goethe's organic relation to life. Their criticism of Bolshevism is strikingly similar to Goethe's criticism of the Jacobins.

Goethe expressed his views on revolution thus:

> And, furthermore, nothing is good for a nation but that which arises from its own core and its own general wants, without apish imitation of another; since what to one race of people, of a certain age, is nutriment, may prove poison for another. All endeavours to introduce any foreign innovation, the necessity for which is not rooted in the core of the nation itself, are therefore foolish; and all premeditated revolutions of the kind are unsuccessful, for they are without God, who keeps aloof from such bungling. If, however, there exists an actual necessity for a great reform amongst a people, God is with it, and it prospers. (Johann Peter Eckermann, *Conversations of Goethe with Johann Peter Eckermann*, trans. John Oxenford [New York: Da Capo Press, 1998], p. 37)

As these brilliant thoughts reveal, Goethe was a gradualist. He uses the word God as a metaphor, the semantic content of which probably includes the paramount good principle in humanity, the worth of life, and high moral qualities leading to universal values. As long as the pulse of such a God beats in them, revolutionary movements do not lapse into despotism and terror.

Gorbachev: You and I understand that humanity—notably Europeans of the 21st century—cannot return to the Greek idea of a static world or live only for the day, enjoying the happiness that nature sends. Awareness of time and hopes for the future entered our flesh and blood with Christianity, and we are unlikely to rid ourselves of them.

With all his expansionism and passion for knowledge, the contemporary human being must study human nature more seriously than before and must penetrate the oneness of nature and humanity with deeper understanding.

Only about twenty years ago, young people insatiably devoured science fiction describing human settlements on other planets like Mars and Jupiter and in other galaxies. Interest in all that has faded. Even space exploration arouses little interest.

Discovery of the impassable limitations on our economic and scientific possibilities is not the only reason for this. Suddenly we have become enormously interested in what we already have. Space flights have revealed not only the limited scale, but also the indescribable beauty of Mother Earth. This indicates that instinctive striving beyond earthly boundaries—beyond the boundaries of what is—is drying up.

The Enlightenment was a philosophy of limitless progress, interpreted as the endless deployment of human strength outward into nature and the cosmos. Interest in the Enlightenment in that sense, too, has dried up.

Ikeda: Faust's monologue just before the onset of the eternal darkness of blindness illustrates the condition you describe:

> My way has been to scour the whole world through.
> Where was delight, I seized it by the hair;
> If it fell short, I simply left it there,
> If it escaped me, I just let it go.
> I stormed through life, through joys in endless train,
> Desire, fulfillment, then desire again;
> Lordly at first I fared, in power and speed,
> But now I walk with wisdom's deeper heed.
> Full well I know the earthly round of men,
> And what's beyond is barred from human ken.
> (Goethe, *Faust*, trans. Philip Wayne [London: Penguin Books, 1959], p. 265)

Constantly and greedily striving for expansion and stopping at nothing, ultimately on the threshold of blindness and death, Faust arrives at a time for calm introspection. His tragedy symbolizes the danger of modern civilization in which arrogance has brought man grave trials.

Admitting ignorance of the will of heaven, Faust is saved at last by Mary the Mater Gloriosa. The last words of the poem, "The Eternal Womanhood leads us above" (Goethe, *Faust*, trans. Philip Wayne, p. 288), reveal how, neutralized by the feminine element, the audacious male principal finds tranquility. Driven as it is by will and ambition, modern civilization, too, clearly needs the kind of pacification that Faust experienced.

Gorbachev: As I see it, Goethe devoted his work to unmasking the superman. At the beginning of the 19th century, most of all in his immortal Faust, he spoke of what Dostoyevsky was to talk of at the end of the same century. The idea is simple and still topical today: "Soul, subdue your impulses!" Goethe spoke of the impossibility of stopping the hands of the clock, though he was untrue to his own claims, for he remained a venial, pleasure-seeking, earthly man until the end of his life.

Ikeda: The main theme of *Faust* is, as you suggest, the unmasking of ambition, like that of Prometheus, who tries to command time and history, just as Faust orders time to stop.

In this connection, I should like to say a few words about the nature of history. The main axis of history is life. The thesis that living is the most important thing is the goal that history must serve. From the historical viewpoint, expansionism and the principle of progressive development failed because their Utopian plan of the future pursued a straight line of progress divided into past, present, and future. According to this scheme, the past and present have no role except to serve the future. Unsurprisingly, such a future flouts history by flinging everything living from its past.

Time must not be interpreted as an inorganic flux bypassing humanity as it moves from past to future. Humanity vitalizes time, and the sense of living time is consonant with the living depths of the human soul.

Gorbachev: My knowledge of my people and our classical literature leads me to say that we Russians have always adopted a cautious attitude toward the ideas of endless linear progress and a ceaseless race to the future.

Herzen protested against Moloch who, while devouring human lives, promises that everything on earth will be fine after their deaths. He wrote: "What am I? I am that which thou hast searched for since thy baby eyes gazed wonderingly upon the world, whose horizon hides this real life from thee." Lev Tolstoy, too, opposed the idea of limitless progress. He did not share the Western view of history and to it opposed the—to him more congenial—Eastern view. In an article on progress, he wrote:

> Common sense tells me that, if a great part of humanity—the so-called East—does not acknowledge, but actually refutes the law of progress, then that law does not exist for all, but only for a part of, humanity. Like all people, I am free of the superstition of progress... and can find no general law in the life of humankind. Subsuming history under the idea of progress is as easy as subsuming it under the idea of regression or of any other historical fantasy that you like. I say further that looking for general laws in history—which is impossible anyway—is needless. The general eternal law is written in the soul of every human being.

Sadly, the laboring masses paid no heed to our great thinkers' warnings. Stalinist socialism lived and acted according to the laws of Herzen's Moloch. Several generations of Soviet people—most of all workers and peasants—labored in poverty and, in the 1930s, in hunger, sacrificing their bellies in the name of a communist future that no one shall ever see.

Ikeda: Berdyaev noted that with each expansion of our consciousness, the past and the future merge into an eternal present. This interpretation of time is very close to the Buddhist understanding.

Buddhism teaches that human life takes place in a continuum passing three stages: past, present, and future. If we want to understand the present, we must look to the causes laid down in the past; and, if we want to know the future, we must look to the causes we are creating in the present. Thus each moment of life is unique and extraordinarily significant. The Lotus Sutra defines "the remote past" (*Kuon*) not as a certain time but as eternal truth, something that is not set in motion but that exists just as it always has, and time is regarded as an unending expanse passing three forms of temporal existence, which we create through our thoughts, words, and deeds as we strive to understand eternal truth.

The Buddhist understanding of history is founded on the unity of these three times. Westerners, in speaking of history, usually have the Christian traditional interpretation in mind—that is, an end connected with the Second Coming of Christ. This is quite distinct from the Buddhist idea.

Buddhism divides history into three periods after the death of Shakyamuni. Each of the periods is called a Day. The first is the Day of the Righteous Law; the second, the Day of the Imitative Law; and the third, the Latter Day of the Law. With transition from the first through the second and into the third, evil intensifies, as the power of the teachings of the Buddha weakens. Buddhism must assume distinctive forms suited to each of these epochs and act with flexibility and circumspection corresponding to the prevailing way of thought. With characteristic wisdom and perspicacity, Buddhism takes into account the circumstances and conditions of each epoch and, in propagating the teachings, foresees the true expectations of the people.

Gorbachev: Your understanding of humanism is similar to mine. We both advocate respect for life and efforts to protect all living things. Many intellectuals—especially in Western Europe—suppose that rejection of modernist ideologies constitutes a new onslaught of conservatism and religious fundamentalism. I should like to explain my interpretation of the new humanism. Theories must be relegated to second place; inherently valuable human life comes first. No theories or ideas justify sacrificing it.

If I may digress for a moment, I should like to relate a memorable dialogue that took place during my visit to Poland in 1990. As I describe in my memoirs, on this occasion, Wojciech Jaruzelski and I met outstanding representatives of Soviet and Polish culture in the newly restored royal palace. In his address to the meeting, Professor Sukhodolsky, a great authority on Polish and European culture, said that life is given to each of us only once. A human being has only one opportunity to experience spiritual happiness and communion with nature. He added that the right to life is sacred and inviolable. There are no goals that justify all means. Surely this approach indicates the choice we must make for the 21st century.

Ikeda: Precisely so. One single life outweighs the world. This must be our 20th-century spiritual behest, to which we must be true in this century. But inevitably we confront age-old evils like war, murder, violence, and terror. Unless we come to grips with them, talk about the value of life will remain empty words; and humanity will regress into debility, idleness, and insignificance.

Gorbachev: To put this topic in the context of the spiritual lessons of the 20th century, I should like to turn our attention to the contradiction inherent in the ideal as a stimulus for progress and improvement. Obviously, without ideals as lamps shedding light in the darkness, there would have been no human history and no modern civilization. But, as history has taught us, faith in ideals has negative as well as positive consequences. This is not always because the ideals become idols. Ideals elevate the soul. Simultaneously, however, they prevent our seeing the world as it is. Unwittingly, Tolstoy himself prepared the spiritual premises for the Bolshevik revolution. Propaganda of even the best-intended ideals leads to the formation of a particular view of the world and indirectly veers away from actual life. We now know that intellectual maximalism and revolutionary extremism were nourished by the idealization of the future and the deification of the ideal society Russia dreamed of—and this was the root of much of our grief.

In a word, we must distinguish between the moral ideal that really stimulates the spiritual development of the individual and gives his or her life greater meaning and the ideological Utopia that provokes violence and destruction.

Ikeda: Primitive or Hinayana Buddhism idealizes the divine world. In the higher Mahayana stage, however, the ideal is understood totally differently. In Mahayana, the barriers between the sacred and the secular no longer exist. Only those who practice Buddhism in the real everyday world can be called truly "enlightened".

Tolstoy raises the question of the dialectic of the ideal in his "Kreutzer Sonata", in which he writes that the higher and more difficult to attain the ideal, the better. The ideal is an ideal when it is attainable only in infinity. Without ideals, satisfaction with what has been attained halts forward motion, thus destroying the possibility of life itself. The ideal is an ideal only when it points out infinite trials and forward leaps in limitless progress and creativity.

Gorbachev: Idolization of the ideal future inevitably led to skepticism about the present, in which millions live. It led to underestimation of the past and of the achievements of the Russian people. In the 19th century, when idealists dominated the intelligentsia, many people became firmly convinced that only those who hate their way of life can become revolutionaries. In this connection, the Revolutionary Catechism of Bakunin and Nechaev—their homily of self-abnegation—is highly instructive:

> The Revolutionary is a doomed person. He has no interests, no affairs, no feelings, no attachments, no property, and not even a name of his own. Everything in him is swallowed up in one exclusive interest, one thought, one passion—revolution. Strict on himself, he must be strict on others. All tender and tenderizing feelings of kin, friendship, love, and gratitude must be crushed by the single cold passion for the revolutionary cause.

The tragedy is that, though we cannot do without ideals, inherent in them is the danger of totalitarianism and violence against life. But in Russia this became clear only after the failure of the communist experiment.

A new, genuine humanism must defend the right of the human being to remain himself and develop his own potentialities. Mechanist humanism put the human being at the apex but, from the outset, digressed from the diversity of human qualities and talents. It despotically demanded that, regardless of abilities, each person become an all-round developed individual capable of replacing God. Such humanism has no sympathy for weak individuals who are incapable of constant, all-round development. It places at the apex, the energetic, even the demonic, person. It is not surprising that the stormy petrel of proletarian revolution, Karl Marx, was himself the product of European humanism.

Ikeda: The social Darwinism of the second half of the 19th century influenced both Marx and Engels. According to its logic, large nations (historic nations in Marx's term) would swallow up small (unhistoric) nations. Colonialism consistent with this logic—even the cruel colonial policies of England in India—was legitimized because it brought progress. Not only Indians, Africans, and Latin Americans, but also the Slavic people were regarded in racist terms. Logically, in the conflict between England and Russia at the end of the 19th century Marx sided with England. Without limiting himself to criticizing Russian politics, Marx frequently spoke scornfully of the Russian people and of Slavs in general. Of course, such comments were not included in Soviet editions of the collected works of Marx and Engels.

Gorbachev: The genuine humanism at the foundation of our new civilization must recognize both the inherent value of human life and the worth of each nation and people. Learning to defend the rights of minorities is insufficient, although democratic strivings to protect minorities from the dictatorship of the majority is one of freedom's greatest achievements. We must understand that minority truths, too, are universal and valuable. Surely the contemplative, peace-loving, harmony seeker has a right to a place beside the man of action.

Ikeda: Buddhism has a saying to the effect that we do not have to alter the nature of the cherry, the apricot, the peach, or the plum. Each brings forth fruit according to its individual natural laws. If there were no trees other than cherries in the world, the cherry would remain undifferentiated. Its individuality appears only when there are plum, peach, and other trees to compare with it. Buddhism opens interior windows through which we can see grass, trees, stones, and even grains of dust as manifestations of the Buddha nature. In this infinite universe, all things serve each other on the mystic basis on which everything depends. The aggregate of countless living and non-living creatures—birds and flowers, the earth and the sun—constitute a symphony of the joy of existence and an embodiment of compassion, to use the words of my own mentor Josei Toda.

Gorbachev: The next trait of what I call the new humanism is connected with genuine pluralism. By this I mean not merely recognizing, but also appreciating the enormous value of the diversity of the world and of human and social qualities. Perestroika started by repudiating Bolshevik uniformity and the elimination of diverse forms of property and class diversity. We were able to take decisive steps in these directions. But exclusivist tendencies and the desire of the powerful to foist their own ideas of truth and beauty on others persist and must be overcome. The Americans want all democracy to be like American democracy. The Western world regards Islamic fundamentalism as a threat. Islam fears total modernization, Westernization, and the loss of the roots of national identity.

How can we learn to be reconciled to the inescapable diversity of our development? History teaches us that humanity has always found it hard to cope with diversity of ideas, arrangements, values, and behavior models. Everything contrary to locally accepted standards has been repudiated or cruelly suppressed. Nonconformism and heresy have always been harshly punished. Diversity has always been regarded as a threat, especially by ruling elites. Consequently, it is difficult to expect respect for diversity to become a fundamental social value all at once. Such a conversion takes time. Nonetheless, I am convinced that diversity will be a major principle of the 21st century and a condition for stable, steady development.

Recognizing and protecting the organic unity of humanity and nature are not enough. We must sacrifice our expansionist strivings in order to protect nature and preserve all her diverse aspects. We must adopt deeper, more serious attitudes toward human nature too.

Ikeda: I share your view completely. Each of the numerous, diverse cultures gracing our planet is unique and has its own view of the world. We must learn to respect the multifaceted nature of our world as it is and adopt the most caring attitudes toward each member of the human community.

To our profound regret, however, human beings often fail to understand the value inherent in each people and each nation, and failure to do so evokes the profoundest regret. In Japan, for instance, the Ainu people and Koreans compelled to live in Japan by militarist colonial policies are still discriminated against. Such things as residential location, educational level, and social position continue to be a basis for discrimination.

Surely the time has come for people to come to their senses. Were we put on earth to hurt each other? We are in the world for only a few decades—an instant in the eternal course of cosmic time. Why should we waste this precious instant of life on tormenting our fellows? As usual, truth is simple: no individual is higher or lower than humanity as a whole. This truth is both our starting point and our destination because it alone ensures an equal right to existence for all.

To safeguard the multifaceted nature of life, we must reject standardized criteria. At present, economic might is the sole measuring stick of the individual and of society. But economy is far from a universal criterion and is not the arbitrator for all members of the human community. Taking a non-economic view reveals the abundance of human diversity. In ecological and family-life cultures, many peoples far outstrip the powers that now rule the world by force.

Our soul hope of survival lies in making a transition from economic and military competition to competition in making contributions to a general fund of humanity. Level of humaneness must become the main criterion by which to judge the extent to which each society is truly civilized. I feel certain the world is headed in that direction.

Gorbachev: The American political scientist Samuel Huntington (1927–) has advocated a theory of war among civilizations. His approach is what college teachers called mechanistic. But over the past few centuries, boundaries have been eroded. Cultures have been energetically interpenetrating. Clear delineations between cultures and civilizations no longer exist. The Russian culture, for instance, is a melding of East and West. Tolstoy is both an Occidental Sage and an Oriental Sage. It seems to me that Huntington's theory makes an absolute out of a particular: the harsh conflict between Islamic fundamentalism and contemporary American culture. There are no cultural conflicts between Russian civilization and the civilizations of China or Japan. Instead of differences, we ought to cultivate respect for what has come into being and justified itself. It is time for humanity to abandon attempts to take nature's place and somehow miraculously restructure humanity. Patently, attempts by contemporary science to penetrate into deep physical structures and to advance from kidney and heart transplants to transplanting the whole human being are fraught with the most destructive consequences.

Science of the 19th and 20th centuries acted and developed in the name of subduing and changing human nature. In the 21st century, science—and most humane learning—must tell us what in human beings does not change and what it is dangerous to alter.

Perhaps we will never delve down to the sources of the conscience and the sense of compassion. But we must preserve and develop all those cultural and spiritual mechanisms that stimulate us to live conscientiously. We may never delve down to the secret of the origin of life. But, clearly, religious reverence for living nature must be the basic imperative of the new humanism. Today, to preserve life and reinforce its diversity we must know the structure, relations, and mechanisms that support human civilization.

We must learn how to cure cancer and AIDS. We must preserve and develop the natural sciences. But we must also learn how to understand that the basic secret is the internal spiritual world of the human being and the laws of its evolution.

Ikeda: People have sometimes discounted Socrates' immortal, phoenix-like words "Know thyself" as outdated and useless. With a know-it-all attitude, they have ignored and flouted them. Tearing along at a breakneck pace, with the most lamentable consequences, people have confused knowledge with wisdom, gullibility with conviction, pleasure with happiness, and productivity with value. When they came to their senses, they were rooted in perplexity in the outer darkness of the end of the 20th century with no idea what to do. In this sense, the 20th— the century of arrogance—might also be called the century of repentance.

Undeniably, psychology—notably child psychology, developmental psychology, and depth psychology—have made great and worthy advances. Unfortunately, the extent to which the development of psychology has added depth to Socrates' words remains highly doubtful. Indeed, the development of learning has further distanced us from wisdom. In the 20th century, people ceased attending to their spiritual worlds and, forgetting themselves, ran around in a vicious circle. Philosophy—the queen of the sciences—first waned then disappeared, leaving a spiritual vacuum behind.

Shutting our ears to the clamor around us, we must heed Goethe's call to remember the greatness of the Greeks and the school of Socrates. He wrote that, from even a brief acquaintance with the dialogues, we immediately understand that Plato, avoiding philosophical jargon, uses everyday examples to dispel distorted ideas imperceptibly. Unlike the loud exclamations of the frivolous, his calm wisdom penetrates to the roots of life.

Towards a New Humanism

Gorbachev: Greek philosophy illuminated the mind without deifying passion and human animal instincts. Only in later times did philosophers begin to give absolute status to hatred, envy, and the instinct for self-destruction. Probably the Greeks knew instinctively that we must not propagandize ideas that undermine faith in humanity. In their profound understanding of human nature and the dangers confronting us, the Greeks were wiser than modern civilizations.

This is what I have in mind when I speak of the general unreproducibility of the human being and his unique qualities. In the 21st century, humanity must be more careful and more circumspect. The new humanism presupposes admiration of courage and of the millions of people who humbly and unpretentiously fulfill their human duties, study, work, bear and raise children, and preserve traditions handed down by their forefathers. We must learn the meaning of life not from people engaged in dialectic mannerisms and mental games that destroy faith, but from those billions of people dead and alive whose lives form the foundation of our own.

Transition to the new humanism and the new civilization presupposes alteration of all the paradigms of human existence. Patently, former mechanical contrasts between socialism and capitalism or liberalism and conservatism are dying out. We must now turn our attention to new conditions and mutual reinforcement of the mechanisms and social instruments that strengthen the primordial bases of life.

Realization of the rights and freedoms of the individual and normal economic growth are impossible without stable government. At the same time, attempts to infringe on civil liberties weaken government by depriving it of life and future prospects.

There is not now nor will there ever be a universal idea capable of solving all the problems confronting humanity. The very universality and interdependence of the world presupposes an inventory and the combination of a multitude of interests and ideas.

We must pay attention to the search for a paradigm integrating all human philosophical and practical achievements, no matter what ideological or political current realized them. The common basis of that paradigm must be universal human values evolved over the ages and the primordial value of human life. The search for a new paradigm must be a search for synthesis, for the things that unite instead of dividing individuals, nations, and peoples.

Ikeda: I agree completely. Everything starts with the first step. Streams form rivers, and rivers flow into seas. Great mountains are made up of small stones. A genuinely peaceful community is the consequence of the deeds of all its members. Consequently, the only reliable way to happiness is conscious self-improvement on the part of the individual. I sincerely hope that the majority of human beings will agree and begin by taking this modest, but extremely courageous first step.

Gorbachev: The 21st will be either a century of total exacerbation of our mortal crisis or a century of purification, spiritual convalescence, and all-round renaissance.

Federico Garcia Lorca wrote that the struggle is among not human, but cosmic forces. He imagined the outcome hanging in a balance before him: on the one side his own pain and sacrifices, on the other justice for all, even if entailing the burdens of transition to an unknown, unguessed future. He concluded that he would bring his own fist down on the side of justice.

I am convinced that all reasonable political forces, all spiritual and ideological currents, and all confessions must promote the transition to the victory of humaneness and justice and help make the 21st a century of renaissance, a century of humanity.

Postscript: From a New Philosophy to a New Politics

Mikhail Gorbachev

The values and mechanism underlying the evolution of contemporary European civilization are on the verge of self-exhaustion. Consumerism and the ceaseless accumulation of capital contradict basic human interests and threaten equilibrium between humanity and the rest of nature. Humankind is unable to halt growing drug addiction, terrorism, and crime. Recent occurrences show us unexpectedly caught up in a new outburst of ethnic wars.

For these reasons, this book's modest attempt to rethink the moral meaning of human experiences in the 20th century—particularly in Russia and Japan—may be useful, at least in stimulating serious reflection on the moral state of contemporary humankind. Mr Ikeda and I are from two different cultures and two different educational backgrounds. Mine is Marxist communist ideology. His is the profundities of Buddhism. Our having discovered a common moral platform is highly significant. Universal human values are a fact and can be a basis for rapprochement and mutual understanding among diverse civilizations. But this can happen only when dialogue participants speak the language of morality, not the language of force and prejudice. The end of the Cold War brought unique possibilities for global rapprochement. They were undervalued and unused first of all because, underestimating the moral meaning of the changes of the time, the West was unable to adopt a moral viewpoint in dialogues with the post-communist world, then awakening to freedom. On the threshold of a new round of geopolitical games, the West was bound hand and foot by egoistical calculations.

I do not want our readers to consider us mere preachers who, ignoring what is under their noses, fail to see the obstacles in the way to what we call the new humanistic civilization. There have already been too many blind egoisms, too many blind ideological biases.

As the majority of our readers will probably agree, it is now time to heal the age-old split between politics and morality. We must realize that the future world must be a world of diversity—many worlds within one world—and that only inner light brings full freedom. At the same time, each of our readers is likely to ask how to achieve peaceful coexistence and cooperation among diverse civilizations. Is there a force that can guarantee the independent development of different cultures? In taking practical steps to resolve conflicts in the post-Cold War world, how are we to avoid monopolism? Who has the right to arbitrate among civilizations? And, most important of all, in principle, can world development be guided?

The ending of the Cold War made our world no safer. Today many people are beginning to look on total Westernization as they once did on the threat of total, forcible communalization. Apparently, the West is incapable of dealing in a reasonable way with the results of the new thinking that freed the world from bloc politics and total confrontation.

The fruits of the new way of thinking—achieved with such difficulty—are withering away before our eyes. Some years ago, Russia rushed towards the West with open arms and the best possible will. But no one in the West followed Russia's example. The West was incapable of working out either a new doctrine of collective security or a new ideology of peaceful development. Today the fate of the world is in the hands of institutes formed during the Cold War. When the Warsaw Pact was deactivated, there was pressing need to create a new system of collective European security. But the European process was sacrificed to old approaches, resulting in the eastward expansion of NATO. Overall, Western defense policy concentrates on how many post-communist countries to include in NATO and when. The possible untoward consequences of this mechanistic approach to the problem of European and global security are overlooked.

This is only one of many examples of how the West, morally and intellectually unprepared for the changes evoked by our new politics, continues along the same old track.

Claims of leadership in a unipolar world, even with the best motivations, provoke people to reject the blessings of democracy. We must consider this before instinctive processes of rejection proceed farther.

Instinctive rejection of new democratic unification—it is tempting to say Westernization—in a new unipolar world may have resulted in more wars than occurred in the old bipolar world, where claims on world dominion were held in restraint. The West assumes that changes in the old Soviet order took place in response to external pressure. Holders of this view would be surprised to learn that the changes were actually manifestations of moral progress on the part of all humanity and, most of all, of peoples no longer able to live the lie of totalitarian ideology.

We must remember that a moral, purely human impulse toward free-dom, universal morality, normal amicable international relations, and elimination of the politics of fear and threats were not signs of Russian political weakness. Respect for personal rights and freedoms played its role. But from this fact people drew the incorrect conclusion that all countries in the post-communist world wanted nothing more than to rush as fast as possible into the "bright American future". Similarly, America's mission was believed by some to consist only in teaching other peoples democracy with all possible haste.

A purely bureaucratic, official approach was taken toward the build-ing of a new democratic civilization. Unfortunately, many Westerners forgot that at the heart of democracy lie those profoundly moral values we have discussed in this book. I mean, first of all, the principle of the moral and political worth of each individual and the principle of toler-ance and respect for the opinions of each individual. I take seriously Mr Ikeda's view that for freedom and democracy to take full force we must renounce violence. Democracy established violently—or, as was the case in Russia in 1993, with the aid of missile attacks—is worth very little. Democracy and double moral standards are incompatible. During the storming of the Moscow White House in October 1993, sacrificing its fundamental principles, the West adopted double moral standards.

I frequently ask myself what will become of forcibly imposed democ-racy when the proponents of force weaken or what will happen to a peace imposed with missiles when the concluders of what they called "agreement" weaken.

I do not doubt the values of democracy or its ability to direct social development in these difficult times. I have been and remain an enemy of authoritarianism and the practice and ideology of the iron hand. Free democratic elections are the only real means of effecting a transi-tion from totalitarianism to democracy. That is why I insisted on the need to conduct parliamentary and presidential elections on time. But, if we are serious about setting up a new humanistic civilization and wish to set forth guidelines and approaches to make it a civilization of diver-sity—worlds within one world—we are obliged to examine critically and revise liberal ideology and democratic institutions too. Human self-knowledge must move in two directions.

In launching Perestroika, we submitted the ideology and practice of communism to pitiless critical analysis. We came to the conclusion that the idea of forcing people to be happy can lead to no good and that the mechanism of moral retribution and the spiritual defeat of violence will sooner or later make themselves known.

In our dialogues, Mr Ikeda and I speak in detail about the moral insolvency of violence and revolutionary extremism. At this point, as a counterbalance to our book's bias toward criticizing communist extremism and communist efforts to remake the world, we must seriously discuss the weaknesses and insufficiencies of Western democratic institutions.

Although communist totalitarianism no longer exists, the crisis of contemporary civilization only deepens. The long-suffering peoples of Bosnia paid dearly for the West's efforts to make each Yugoslavian republic an independent presidential republic. Important international decisions on Yugoslavia were made without taking into account the specifics of its complicated makeup or the history of the Serbian people as the prevailing ethnic group in the region. The UN was compelled to take measures involving massive bombardment of the Bosnian Serbs. But the West was unprepared to conduct qualitative peace-making missions. After agreements were signed, the Croatian–Muslim confederation showed signs of splitting.

In the new unipolar world, the fate of peoples once again depends on prevailing moods among the officials of the United States, the leader of world democracy—even on presidential election campaigns. In 1995, after the deaths of thousands of peaceful Bosnians, the Dayton Peace Accord made a decision that good sense and the history of the religiously divided Serbs suggested from the very outset. I am convinced that the Yugoslavian tragedy would never have occurred if, instead of hurrying to recognize the independence of Croatia and Slovenia and later of Bosnia and Herzegovina, the West had held a preliminary international peace conference to convince the conflicting national parties to compromise and discuss the rights of then emerging national minorities. But they were all in a rush to punish the Serbian communists as fast as possible. They were in a hurry to push the Yugoslavian peoples along the road to democracy.

Once again ideological passions took pride of place. The ideological approach to world politics was revived because the reasons and motivations behind the new way of thinking and behind our initiatives to end the Cold War were not objectively and honestly evaluated. We did not abandon our own ideological approach in order to become slaves of a new ideology or the students and novices of Milton Friedman and Friedrich August von Hayek. We rejected the ideological approach in the name of the moral approach.

The very principles and institutions of democracy—most of all American democracy—require critical examination. Western attempts to turn Bosnia into America and to hold elections in an ethnically divided land led to tragedy. Elementary considerations were ignored.

For instance, Bosnian Serbs who fought the Turkish yoke for five centuries cannot live in a land with a Muslim president. Even in Africa, liberated from colonialism, new public history did not start from scratch. The peoples of the Balkans have millennia of public history. Similar factors went unconsidered when the international community supported the collapse of the Soviet Union. But thousands of years of history cannot be so easily overlooked.

Many scholars and politicians in the West and even in the United States advance a full barrage of serious arguments questioning American claims to ideological and political leadership. In the first place, the United States is not rich enough to subsidize endless democracy-supporting programs that, as a rule, have effects opposite to those intended. Bursting at the seams, the national budget cannot even provide medical insurance for the poor and aged. Second, the United States is far from a suitable object of emulation in several respects. Ethnic and racial conflicts that the United States tries to resolve in other countries remain unsolved at home. The Black demonstration called the March of Millions that took place in Washington in 1995 showed once again that smoldering racial conflicts still hinder basic solutions to overcome the split between Black and White America. Third, as they themselves sometimes say, Americans are incapable of coming to grips with realities conflicting with their tremendous overload of myths and misconceptions about their own country. The average American has only the vaguest idea of other cultures and histories. This ignorance provides unique opportunities for the manipulation of public opinion. Fourth, in America, the fourth estate—the mass media—have inordinate power. They make presidents and destroy them as politicians. The overwhelming majority of the American people are busy trying to earn their daily bread and must be satisfied with world views concocted by the electronic information media. Consequently, public opinion trends and the entire course of political events depend on the honesty and probity of the people controlling the mass-media empire. Only a new, global cultural revolution making each individual an aware subject of world politics can counteract the expanding omnipotence of the fourth estate.

We must realize that, in spite of great 20th-century successes in mass education, humanity still has not solved the major problems set by the great educators. Even in the most advanced nations, including the United States, the popular humanitarian cultural level is extremely low. Increasing drug addiction and criminality testify to the pathological condition of the human spirit and a lack of spirituality and humaneness. The gap between the uneducated and the educated parts of society widens. Under such conditions, millions of people remain the objects of inconceivable political manipulation. Although the United States has assumed the burden of leading contemporary democratic civilization, it too is equally affected by all these problems.

The problems and contradictions of the political system in the United States, the outpost of Western democracy, is only one example endorsing our thesis that it is time for a reexamination of contemporary liberal civilization as a whole.

But, even as we begin discussing this topic, we must think of ways to avoid new world unification. The problems of global security can be resolved only when all nations today assume collective responsibility for the future of humanity. I use the word "security" in a broad sense, including economic, ecological, and informational as well as military security.

Realizing that all projects for the creation of global government are myths, we must begin improving already existing international organizations, notably the United Nations. UN power and ability to overcome international conflicts is of primary concern. Its peace-making efforts in Bosnia showed up all its weaknesses. First is its poverty and decisive dependence on the United States. Second is the nature of the Security Council. In dealing with peace-keeping operations, its members are guided first and foremost by their own national preferences and by efforts to support one side or another. This intensifies and aggravates the conflict under consideration.

What does all this lead us to conclude? To have a future, the United Nations must become a genuinely independent, financially strong organization capable of conducting policies motivated by the global security of all human civilization. Changing economic and military might of member nations and certain basic civilization principles necessitate expansion of the Security Council. I say this for these reasons. If we intend to create a new, diverse, humanistic civilization that is, as I say, worlds within one world, the Security Council itself must be a world of worlds. Representatives of all existing civilizations—without exception—must have the right to influence Security Council decisions which in any way concern the general security of humanity.

As members of the United Nations, sovereign states have consistently put their own national interests above everything. The civilized approach to defining the UN that I have just outlined would enable the Security Council gradually to become more than an organization of sovereign states and to make decisions in the interests of humanity as a whole. The problem of cooperation between the UN and regional organizations too might be put in terms of this same kind of civilized relationship.

There is another problem connected with both improving UN action and the theme of our book. I mean UNESCO. If humanity is being more and more united, why not devise guidelines for a system of humanitarian education based on the moral experience of all humankind and the moral wisdom of all religions? Ultimately, we might write a textbook on world history relating not wars but moral deeds. (Ironically, the *Washington Post* opened its competition for the most outstanding figure in the second millennium with an essay on Genghis Khan.)

Today we must consider a wider problem: the cultural reorientation of all human civilization and a new moral and cultural reformation.

Postscript: The Crisis of Human Dignity

Daisaku Ikeda

This dialogue had a great emotional impact on me. Mr Gorbachev was once the supreme leader of a nation with an official philosophy of rejecting religion. Being able to conduct totally free conversations extending to inner religious truths with such a man made me experience once again the panoramic drama of his period in power.

I recognize the great significance of having as a dialogue partner a man of rare caliber and the embodiment of the new thinking. When we met at Soka University a number of years ago, he frankly said that any consideration of the 21st century must include the world of religion. In the course of our dialogue, I have become certain that this insistence emerged from his nature as a great reformer.

Tragic, disheartening events of the past several years have prompted a split in opinion about the very nature of historical progress. In this dialogue, we repeatedly express the opinion that union is good and separation evil. Taking this as a guideline, I interpret events since the fall of the Berlin Wall as regression in world history. In spite of its pessimistic tone, Francis Fukuyama's *The End of History*, published in 1992, proclaimed the victory of capitalism over socialism. In Japan especially it aroused welcome anticipations that totalitarian regimes would tumble like dominos. Writers dashed off a spate of optimistic works about the acceleration of democratization. For the most part, however, they were not cool analyses, but rose-tinted, faintly optimistic observations. Whatever points liberal society had scored resulted not from its own victories but from the enemy's errors. Though this became perfectly clear, liberals mistakenly took credit and rejoiced without looking where they were going. The merciless events of later history destroyed the flimsy grounds of their optimism. The vision of a new order following the brilliant victory of the Gulf War was soon washed away in the current of the times, leaving not a wrack behind.

The avalanche that swept the former Soviet Union and other socialist countries in the last decade of the 20th century was not a superficial triumph of Western-style liberalism and democracy. It was an event of global significance that we must judge deeply and with a long-term view. We must not consider it something that can happen only elsewhere. By its very nature, it cannot be explained in easy-to-grasp, black-or-white dualities like victory and defeat.

We must first examine its meaning for the whole world. We must coolly and earnestly try to find out and cope with the relations between it and our own position. We must modestly lend an ear when wise Russian leaders, like Mikhail Gorbachev, explain what compelled them to choose Perestroika and the new way of thinking. Taking into consideration differences in ethnic and historical background, we must adopt the proper stance of advise and cooperate.

Russian leaders abandoned the ideological approach in order to blaze a path to the moral approach embodied in the new way of thinking. They had no intention of abandoning one ideology in order to become the slaves of another. In this light, it is easy to understand how the United States irritated them.

The traditional American tendency is to judge right and wrong ideologically. Americans tend to grow heated in both good and bad senses over ideas like liberty, democracy, and human rights. Since the American Revolution, they have regarded themselves as keepers of the ideals and, at the same time, as world police. The tendency grew especially pronounced in the 20th century. But, confronted with the complexities of reality, the clear-cut, rectilinear, ideological American approach often results in misapplications. In the second half of the 20th century, diplomacy based on it caused mistakes and setbacks especially in relation to Third World countries with different traditions. The Vietnam War is a searing example.

The classical Wild West movie embodied what might be called the "cowboy" philosophy: the Indians are the bad guys and the American cavalrymen the good guys. Although such movies have gone out of fashion now, their imprint on mental attitudes lingers.

The American ideological approach strove to force a Soviet Union in transition to a market economy into a textbook mold. At the end of the Cold War, the American sociologist Immanuel Wallerstein much more accurately described conditions when he said that the events of 1989 witnessed the end of both Leninism and the Western interpretation of the historical process. (Incidentally, amid the triumphant celebrations at the end of the Gulf War, Wallerstein made the disquieting, as it turned out to be accurate, prediction that within six months the confetti would be only a bitter memory for unemployed returnee military personnel.)

Clearly, retribution for arrogant intoxication with the superiority of capitalism and liberalism was not long coming in the form of a fast and violent winnowing at the end of the century. The former socialist states that had rushed to break from stagnation and embrace a new epoch found themselves betrayed by Western trappings and values. Despairing and disoriented, they reached an impasse. This is scarcely surprising because behind the material abundance of liberal society in the West and Japan lurks a pathological condition. Money worship, hedonism, and secularism do not bring true happiness and fulfillment or create the real image of a universally appealing society. Liberalism and democracy have seriously hollowed out. Liberal society is now at the critical stage where its values cannot be rehabilitated without fundamental reevaluation.

Like England in the 19th century, America was the world leader in the 20th century. But, by the end of the century, a dark cloud began dimming the luster of formerly brilliant phrases such as "American way of life", "American mind", "American dream", and "American democracy". All around us, thinkers point out the decline of the sole remaining superpower. The American mind is said to be closed. The American century is said to be over. Americanization has stopped, and America is splitting. People ask why. Symbolized by the American condition, the contemporary civilizational crisis goes far deeper than confrontation or the relative merits and demerits of liberalism and socialism. It plumbs a depth requiring consideration of modern civilization in terms of centuries.

Our crisis is not one of system, but of humanity itself—in short, it is a crisis of human dignity. I believe a keen appreciation of this led Mr Gorbachev and his team to reject the ideological for the moral approach.

To make real progress in creating a better society we must recognize and cope with a whole complex of practical problems including deterioration of the environment, regional economic development, and the exhaustion of energy sources and food. But, as a Buddhist, I realize that, unless we deal with inner human pollution, none of our efforts to solve such external problems can have any effect.

In spite of our superficially brilliant contemporary civilization, human beings seem petty and wretched. Obsessed by pleasure, convenience, and efficiency they follow wherever their desires lead. Increasingly egotistical, they fall into self-set traps of money-worship and hedonism. Disdainful of what transcends themselves, they are confined within narrow boundaries of secularism. They are isolated from the universe and the world of nature and incapable of proudly and vociferously proclaiming their own humanity, as Walt Whitman does in "Song of Myself": "Walt Whitman, a kosmos, of Manhattan the son."

Whitman was a man on a grand scale. Adam Smith developed the idea of another kind of man—economic man (*homo economicus*)—and constructed his own system of economics on the recognition of human selfishness. Unlike the modern economic animal, however, Smith's economic man pursues profit on the basis of selfishness and compassion guided by the rationality of a divine plan tending to the general welfare. For Smith, the path to wealth is under the guidance of God's invisible hand and is related to the path to virtue. Characteristics of Smith's economic man are frugality, diligence, thrift, caution, scrupulousness, promptness, consistency, and reliability. The intensely ethical image conjured up by these traits differs entirely from the modern economic animal (not necessarily confined to the world of finance), who is shrewd at profit–loss calculations and nothing else. Smith insists that egoism and self-love must be rendered maturely humane through education and cultivation. His economic man is distinctly free of the vanities of hedonism and money-worshipping distinctive of the modern version.

I welcomed the collapse of the Cold War structure as indicative of the will of the people and the current of democratization. But I had apprehensions about making these things last. Cultivation and tempering of the inner lives of the masses are essential to the advance of democracy. And in this connection, the outlook was unknown.

In my annual SGI Day peace proposal in early 1990, referring to Plato's criticism of democracy, I addressed the issue of the structure of the inner world, without the cultivation of which the masses of the people are in jeopardy.

In his astute analysis of American democracy, Alexis de Tocqueville wrote that, whereas feudal society had been stable, in the age of democracy, with its slogans of freedom and equality, everything is in flux. The human mind is the least stable of all. It is impossible to expect a stable, wholesome, popular government without popular mental stability because unchecked egoism results only in mob rule.

Plato was skeptical about democracy because mob rule in the name of Athenian democracy had taken the life of his revered teacher Socrates. In *The Republic*, he ranks political systems in the following order: (1) aristocracy, (2) timocracy, (3) oligarchy, (4) democracy, and (5) tyranny. Democracy ranks only fourth and, because of its fatal internal contradictions, inevitably leads to tyranny. Bertrand Russell and other modern defenders of democracy have rejected this evaluation. But, after 2,000 years, I believe that we must not disregard Plato's concern and skepticism as unfounded. Reversals in the post-Cold War age of the popular will and the current of democratization suggest he was right.

Affording preeminence to the inner human world, I should like to go somewhat further into what Plato says in *The Republic* about democracy and its transition into tyranny. Advocates of democracy, says Plato, argue that freedom is the greatest virtue of democracy and that, therefore, a democracy is the only state suitable to human beings, whose nature is essentially free. Yet by supporting the insatiable pursuit of freedom, democracy nurtures a multitude of desires that gradually and insidiously "seize the citadel at the young man's soul" and lead him down the path of conceit. Modesty is dismissed as silliness, temperance is shamed as unmanly, and moderation and orderly expenditure are called boorish and mean. And the throng celebrates, "having garlands on their heads, and a great company with them, hymning their praises and calling them by sweet names; insolence they term breeding, and anarchy liberty, and waste magnificence, and impudence courage". Finally, the situation gets out of control and a strong leader is sought to restore order. From among the "idle drones", a single stinger-equipped creature is chosen, who at first emerges as the leader of the masses, but who soon gives in to the diabolical lure of power, and is inevitably transformed into a tyrant. And so, as Plato astutely points out: "The excess of liberty, whether in States or individuals, seems only to pass into excess slavery in the hands of a dictator."

It is essential to remember that, in *The Republic*, Plato's primary area of interest is a theory, not of systems but of humanity. It deals with human internal politics. His efforts to illuminate the eternal human riddle and his extraordinary literary talent keep his works forever new and make them compellingly pertinent to the political conditions of our own times. Though sometimes confusing, his Socratic dialogues continue to appeal and stimulate reflection on basic human themes, including simple everyday matters and greater issues like the nature of true happiness and the way people ought to live.

The highly influential American journalist Walter Lippmann insisted on the importance of Socratic methods to the development and maturation of democracy. In the United States, the mass media control public opinion, which in turn plays a definitive role in American society and democracy. In his notable book *Public Opinion*, Lippmann warned against a public opinion that can be misread as a result of stereotypes created by the mass media, and stressed the importance of Socratic dialogue and Socratic people in preventing this. As we witness the regression of all—not just American—democracy, we realize that Lippmann's call for the people to be wise has increased in significance.

Buddhist scriptures say that a person who cannot manage to cross a moat 10 feet wide, will never be able to cross one that is 100 or 200 feet wide (*WND*, p.766). They also say that a 1,000-mile journey starts with one step. In other words, the most assiduous efforts will fail unless we first deal with what is under our noses. The Socratic dialogue always deals with the immediate. This is why the attitude it represents is essential to the revitalization of democracy and optimism about the future.

In Plato's *Gorgias*, the spirited Athenian politician Callicles ridicules Socrates' admonitions to temperance: "luxury, intemperance, and license, if they be provided with means, are virtue and happiness". Gently turning aside this hot-blooded bragging and employing his celebrated question-and-answer (maieutic) method, Socrates pinpoints the contradictions of Callicles' hedonism. Socrates supposes that there is a person with an itch who spends his whole life scratching it, and asks whether such a person can be said to have lived happily. Callicles is immediately perplexed. They are dealing with the question of whether living pleasurably is the same thing as living happily—whether a comfortable life is a good life. The dialogue then develops at Socrates' pace. One wonders whether today's money-worshippers and hedonists would lend an ear to the words of a sage as candidly as Callicles listened to Socrates.

Like Socrates, Shakyamuni combined compassion and wisdom in guiding people to the right attitudes toward life. On one occasion, a grieving woman asked him for a medicine that would restore her recently deceased child to life. Saying that he knew the way, he told her to bring him a white poppy seed from a house where no one had ever died. Carrying her dead child on her back, she set out on the search. But every house she visited had experienced death. When night fell without her having obtained the poppy seed, she thought: "I've been considering only the death of my own child, but as I've walked all over town, I've come to see that there are more dead than living." Gradually the woman grieved less and less and finally returned to Shakyamuni and became enlightened to basics like the inconstancy of life, the inevitability of death for all living creatures, and the Four Sufferings—birth, aging, illness, and death.

The theme and dream of my life are to cultivate the use of the dialogue methods of Socrates and Shakyamuni as far as possible and on the maximum number of levels. No matter how circuitous it may seem, this path is the righteous way to breakthroughs in the contemporary impasse of our times. And I intend to pursue it. I also believe that this way connects with Mr Gorbachev's determination to stimulate individual cultural revolutions all over the world in the hope of cultivating citizens capable of thinking for themselves.

I fully realize that the task is difficult. Inconsistent words and popularity-seeking will not serve the purpose. In Socrates' own day, the Sophists lectured and taught for money and fame. Socrates himself was accused of corrupting the youth, mistakenly criticized, slandered, and finally put to death. But history is a stern judge. And there is need to ask whose words—those of Socrates or those of the Sophists—embody profound observation and assertions of humanity. The words of the person who, in spite of all criticism, injury, and even threat of death, remains true to his ideals carry real weight. My own mentor Josei Toda always said that words without faith are like smoke. The memory of this timeless statement remained with me throughout my dialogue of faith with Mr Gorbachev.

In conclusion, as my numerous peace proposals make clear, I am in complete agreement with his ideas about the United Nations. Ensuring the organization a brilliant future depends on the extent to which we are able to strengthen its soft-power aspects. At present, centered on the Security Council, it overstresses hard-power. Although military force will probably remain essential in settling international disputes, it is doubtful that we can reestablish order by veering too far in that direction. World conditions following the Gulf War—especially in Bosnia—demonstrated the limitations of hard-power. Instead of following that course, the United Nations, as a council of humanity, must first of all activate systems and rules founded on dialogue and debate. As a nongovernmental organization member of the UN, we of SGI are eager to do our part in this undertaking.

Glossary

Aitmatov, Chingiz	(1928–), author, translator and journalist; formerly a Pravda correspondent in Kyrgyz
Ajatashatru	a king in India in the time of Shakyamuni Buddha who converted to Buddhism out of remorse for his evil acts
Aleksandr II	(1818–81), liberator of the serfs, Tsar of Russia during the Crimean War
Amida Buddha	the Buddha of the Pure Land of Perfect Bliss
anti-semitism	term coined in 1879 to express hostility toward or discrimination against Jews as a religious or racial group
archbishop	a Christian bishop with authority in his own diocese and jurisdiction over other bishops in his archdiocese
Armenia	country south of the Caucasus mountain range, facing the northwestern extremity of Asia
Azerbaijan	country south of the Caucasus, populated by Iranian speakers, nomadic Turkic tribes, Kurds and Christian Albanians
Balkan Peninsula	easternmost peninsula in Europe; containing Slovenia, Croatia, Bosnia and Herzegovina, Serbia and Montenegro, Macedonia, Albania, Bulgaria, Romania and Moldova
Belarus	smallest of three Slavic republics of the former Soviet Union, independent since 1991, capital city Minsk
Belinsky, Vissarion G.	(1811–48), eminent Russian literary critic
Belovezh Agreement	the December 1991 agreement disbanding the USSR and establishing the CIS
Berdyaev, Nikolai	(1874–1948), religious thinker, philosopher and Marxist who became a critic of Russian implementation of Karl Marx's views
Bergson, Henri	(1859–1941), French philosopher who elaborated a process philosophy rejecting static

	values in favor of values of motion, change and evolution
Bimbisara	an Indian king, who was imprisoned and killed by his son, Ajatashatru; a devout follower of Shakyamuni Buddha
Bolsheviks	the wing of the Russian Social Democratic Workers' Party, led by Lenin, which seized control of the Russian government in October, 1917
Brzezinski, Zbigniew	US national security advisor, 1977–81
Bulgakov, Sergei	(1871–1944), economist and Russian Orthodox theologian who developed a philosophical system stressing the unity of all things
Bunin, Ivan A.	(1870–1953), poet and novelist, first Russian to receive the Nobel Prize for Literature (1933)
Bushido	originally the code of conduct of the samurai, made the basis of ethical training for Japanese society in the mid-19th century
capitalism	economic system in which the means of production are privately owned and income is distributed through the operation of markets
Caucasus	a mountain system in Russia, encompassing Georgia, Azerbaijan and Armenia
Chaliapin, Fyodor Ivanovich	(1873–1938) Russian opera singer
Chechnya	European republic in SE Russia on the north slope of the Caucasus Mountains
Cold War	ideological conflict between the US and the USSR
Comintern	Communist International, established in 1919 and dissolved in 1943
Communist Manifesto	1848 pamphlet written by Karl Marx and Friedrich Engels which became a principal programmatic statement for European communist parties in 19th and 20th centuries
Cousins, Norman	(1915–90), American essayist and *Saturday Review* editor
Crimea	autonomous republic in southern Ukraine
Day of the Imitative Law	also Middle Day of the Law, the second of the three consecutive periods following

Shakyamuni's death, in which the Buddha's teaching gradually becomes formalized and progressively fewer people attain enlightenment through its practice

Day of the Righteous Law also Former Day of the Law, the first of the three consecutive periods following Shakyamuni's death, when the Buddha's teaching and practice still remain, and proof of their efficacy, in the form of many people attaining enlightenment, continues

dependent origination a Buddhist doctrine expressing the interdependence of all things

Devadatta a cousin of Shakyamuni Buddha, first his disciple and later his enemy; the subject of the twelfth chapter of the Lotus Sutra

Don river and vital artery in the European portion of Russia

Dostoyevsky, Fyodor (1821–81), Russian novelist and short-story writer, famous for psychological insights into the darkest recesses of the human heart

Einstein, Albert (1879–1955), German–Swiss–US scientist, former patent examiner, theoretical physicist, noted for his Theory of Relativity, and an advocate for nuclear disarmament

Emerson, Ralph Waldo (1803–82), American lecturer, poet and essayist; leading exponent of American Transcendentalism

Faust hero of western folklore who sells his soul to the devil in exchange for knowledge and power

February Revolution the first of two revolutions in Russia in 1917 which overthrew the imperial government

Fourier, Charles (1772–1837), French social theorist who advocated a reconstruction of society based on communal associations of producers

Garcia-Lorca, Federico (1898–1936), Spanish poet and dramatist; shot without trial by fascists during the Spanish Civil War

Georgia Republic former Soviet state, a member of the Commonwealth of Independent States since 1991

Glasnost the Soviet policy of open discussion of political and social issues, instituted by Mikhail Gorbachev in the late 1980s

Goethe, Johann Wolfgang	(1749–1832), German poet, novelist, playwright and natural philosopher
Gomulka, Wladislaw	(1905–82), leader of the Polish Communist Party
Gorbachev Foundation	activities center on humanitarian aid; primarily funded by royalties and lecture fees donated by Mikhail Gorbachev
Green Cross International	promotes legal, ethical and behavioral norms regarding the environment; resolves conflicts arising from environmental degradation; provides assistance to people affected by environmental consequences of war and conflict
Havel, Václav	(1936–), Czech playwright, poet and political dissident; president of Czechoslovakia 1989–92, president of Czech Republic 1993–2003
Hegel, Georg Wilhelm Friedrich	(1770–1831), German philosopher who developed a dialectical scheme that emphasized the progress of history and ideas from thesis to anti-thesis to synthesis
Hinduism	the beliefs, practices and socio-religious institutions of the Hindus, originally the inhabitants of the land of the Indus River
holocaust	the systematic, state-sponsored killing of six million Jewish men, women and children by Nazi Germany and its collaborators during World War II
Human Revolution, The	the process of self-development and self-realization accomplished through compassionate Buddhist activities; title of the fictionalized history of Soka Gakkai written by Daisaku Ikeda
Huntington, Samuel	(1927–), US political scientist
Iron Curtain	political, military and economic barrier by which the Soviet Union sealed itself and its dependent allies from open contact with the West
Jacobinism	the faction of the French Revolution identified with extreme egalitarianism and violence and the "reign of terror"
Jaruzelski, Wojciech	(1923–), army general and communist

	leader of Poland, chief of state 1981–89, president 1989–90
Kadar, Janos	(1912–89), Hungarian premier 1956–58, 1961–65; played a key role in the transition from anti-Soviet government to pro-Soviet regime; responsible for withdrawal of Soviet troops and restoration of internal independence
KGB	Soviet agency responsible for intelligence, counter-intelligence, and internal security
Khruschev, Nikita	(1894–1971), Soviet premier 1953–64 whose policy was de-Stalinization and peaceful coexistence with capitalist countries
Kiev	the capital of Ukraine and a port city
kolkhoz system	the Stalinist policy of replacing individual farms with collective farms
Komsomol	USSR organization for young people aged between 14 and 28; primarily a political organ to teach Communism
Kosygin, Aleksei	(1904–1980), Soviet premier 1964–80, known as a pragmatic economic administrator
Kremlin	a fortified enclosure at the heart of Moscow from the 15th century; a symbol of Russian and Soviet power
Kurskaya Duga	World War II battleground near the Don River where more than 360,000 soldiers were killed, wounded or captured
Kyrgyz Republic	newly independent nation in Central Asia, formerly known as Kyrgyzstan
Latter Day of the Law	the last of the three consecutive periods following the death of Shakyamuni Buddha, during which his teachings become muddled and lose their efficacy
Lenin, Vladimir Ilich	(1870–1924), founder of the Russian Communist Party; leader of the Russian Revolution of 1917
Liberal-Democratic Party	a Japanese political party, formally inaugurated in 1955 when the merging of three parties made it the largest single party in Japanese history; it maintained a majority in the Lower House until 1993
Lotus Sutra	the text central to the Tendai and Nichiren

	sects of Mahayana Buddhism
Mahatma Gandhi	(1869–1948), leader of the Indian nationalist movement against British rule, esteemed for his doctrine of nonviolent protest; Mahatma is a designation meaning "Great Soul"; his birth name was Mohandas Karamchand Gandhi
Mahayana Buddhism	one of the two major streams of Buddhism (the other being Hinayana); it is distinguished by an emphasis on the virtue of compassion
Makiguchi, Tsunesaburo	(1871–1944), founder-president of Soka Gakkai, author of *Education for Creative Living* and *A Geography of Human Life*
Maksimov, Vladimir	(1932–), dissident novelist and poet
Maoism	a variation of Marxism and Leninism developed by Mao Zedong, it substitutes the agrarian peasantry for the Marxist-Leninist proletariat that China did not have
Marcel, Gabriel	(1889–1973), French philosopher, dramatist and critic
Marx, Karl	(1818–83), German political philosopher, economic theorist, and revolutionary
Matthew	one of the Twelve Apostles, author of the first Gospel, lived in the 1st century AD
Maurois, André	(1885–1967), born Emile Herzog, French novelist and biographer
McCarthyism	the persecution of persons in the US accused of being communists; begun by Senator Joseph R. McCarthy (1908–57)
Meiji period	reign of the Meiji emperor (1868–1912) in Japan; a time of rapid modernization and westernization
More, Sir Thomas	(1478–1535), humanist, statesman, and chancellor of England; beheaded for refusal to recognize King Henry VIII as head of the Church of England
Morse, Edward S.	(1838–1925), US zoologist, active in Japan in Meiji period; awarded Order of the Rising Sun; famous for Japanese pottery collection now owned by the Boston Museum of Fine Arts
Mosaic Law	the first five books of the Bible's Old

	Testament, traditionally ascribed to Moses who was the recipient of God's guidance to humanity; called the Torah in Judaism
mullah	Muslim title applied to scholars or religious leaders
muzhik	nickname for the Russian peasant
narodnik	a member of the 19th-century socialist movement in Russia which believed that propaganda among the peasants would lead to the awakening of the masses
New Testament	the second of the two books of the Christian Bible; considered to be the fulfillment of the promises of the Old Testament
New Thinking	policies of openness (Glasnost) and restructuring of authority (Perestroika) initiated by Mikhail Gorbachev in the 1980s
Nichiren Daishonin	(1222–82), Japanese Buddhist prophet, founder of Nichiren Buddhism which reveres the teachings of the Lotus Sutra
Nichiren sect	school of Buddhism practicing the teachings of Nichiren Daishonin
Nicholas II	(1868–1918), last Russian empereror who, together with his family, was killed by the Bolsheviks
Old Testament	written between 1200 and 100 BC, it is an account of God's dealings with the Hebrew people; it tells of the Israelites settling in the Promised Land, the messages of the prophets, theology, and additional history
Ortega y Gasset, José	(1883–1955), Spanish philosopher who greatly influenced Spain's 20th-century cultural and literary renaissance
Ottoman Empire	named for Osman I (1259–1326), a Turkish Muslim prince in Bythnia; it prospered from 1345 until the Battle of Lepanto in 1571; once the world's largest empire, it was dissolved through post-World War I treaties and was abolished when Turkey became a republic in 1922 under Mustafa Kemal Ataturk
Pasternak, Boris	(1890–1960), Russian poet and prose writer, author of *Doctor Zhivago* (1957); awarded the

	Nobel Prize for Literature in 1958 but unable to accept it owing to Soviet politics
Pauling, Linus	(1901–94), noted for his studies on molecular structure and chemical bonding; awarded the Nobel Prize for Chemistry (1954) and the Nobel Peace Prize (1962) for his efforts on behalf of nuclear weapons control
Perestroika	the program to restructure Soviet political and economic policy and reduce Communist Party involvement in governance; initiated by Mikhail Gorbachev in the 1980s
Peter I	(1672–1729), tsar of Russia, also called Peter the Great; one of Russia's greatest statesmen, organizers, and reformers
Plato	(*c*.427–347 BC), Greek philosopher taught by Socrates and teacher of Aristotle, the three men who laid the foundations of western culture
Politburo	created in 1917 as the supreme policy-making body of the Communist Party, dissolved in 1991
Prague Spring	brief period of liberalization in Czechoslovakia in 1968 under Alexander Dubcek
Prometheus	one of the Titans and a god of fire in Greek mythology; said to have stolen fire from the gods and given it to humans
Proudhon, Pierre-Joseph	(1809–1865), French journalist and socialist whose anarchism was attacked by Karl Marx
Pugachev, Emilian	(1744–75), a Don Cossack, leader of the Pugachev Rebellion (1773–75)
Pushkin, Aleksandr S.	(1799–1837), Russian writer, leading poet of the romantic school, founder of modern Russian literature; representative works include *Boris Godunov*, *Eugene Onegin*, and *The Bronze Horseman*
rabbi	a person qualified by scriptural studies to serve as the spiritual leader of a Jewish community
Razin, Stepan (Stenka)	(1630–71), Russian Cossack rebel and folk hero, immortalized in songs and legends
Robespierre	(1758–94), French revolutionary, leader of

	the Jacobins, virtual dictator during France's Reign of Terror
Rostov	west-central Russian city dating from 862
Rostov-on-Don	port and industrial center in southern Russia since 1749; extensively damaged in World War II
Russian Orthodox Church	Russia's de facto national church since 988; its administration was made a department of state under Tsar Peter I, then suppressed under Soviet rule; resurgent since 1991
Rybakov, Anatoly	(1911–98), Russian author whose novels of life under Stalin were popularized after Glasnost in the 1980s
Sakharov, Andrei Dmitriyevich	(1921–89), Russian nuclear physicist and human rights advocate
sangha	(also samgha), the community of Buddhist believers
Schweitzer, Albert	(1875–1965), Alsatian-born German theologian, philosopher, organist and mission doctor; famous for his "reverence for life" principle; awarded the Nobel Peace Prize in 1952
Sermon on the Mount	biblical collection of religious teachings attributed to Jesus Christ; reported in the Gospel of Matthew and regarded as the blueprint for a Christian life; replaces the law of retribution with a new law of love
Shakyamuni	also called Gautama Buddha, given name Siddhartha; founder of Buddhism whose highest teachings are preserved in the Lotus Sutra; opinions on dates of birth and death differ, 560–480 BCE seems probable
Shintoism	indigenous religious beliefs and practices of Japan vying with Buddhism
Siberia	region of north-central Asia, largely in Russia, extending from the Ural Mountains to the Pacific Ocean, and from the Arctic Ocean to the boundaries of China and Mongolia; site of forced labor camps in Stalinist era
social Darwinism	the theory that persons, groups and races are subject to the same laws of natural selection

	as plants and animals in nature
socialism	the system of social organization in which private property and the distribution of income are subject to social control
Socrates	(470–399 BC), Greek philosopher whose way of life, character and thought profoundly influenced ancient and modern philosophy; noted for philosophical conversations based on a series of probing questions, a pedagogical technique known as the Socratic method
Soka Gakkai	a lay religious organization founded in Japan in 1930 and formally inaugurated in 1937; the society follows the teachings of Nichiren, based on the Lotus Sutra's philosophy of compassion
Solidarity	Polish trade union founded in 1980, with Lech Walesa as its chairman; it won economic reforms and the right to free elections
Solovyov, Vladimir	(1853–1900), Russian philosopher and mystic who attempted a synthesis of religious philosophy, science and ethics in the context of universal Christian unity
Solzhenitsyn, Aleksandr I.	(1918–), Russian novelist and historian, author of *Cancer Ward* (1968) and *The Gulag Archipelago* (1973); awarded the Nobel Prize for Literature (1970)
Stalin, Joseph	(1879–1953), Soviet politician and dictator; noted for a policy of five-year plans that radically altered social structures and resulted in the death of millions
Stalingrad	site of an unsuccessful German assault in World War II marking the farthest extent of the German advance
Stalinism	the policies of Joseph Stalin in the USSR and his imitators in other Soviet bloc countries
Stavropol	city in southwestern Russia on the northern flank of the Greater Caucasus, founded in 1777
syncretism	the fusion of diverse religious beliefs and practices
Tagore, Rabindranath	(1861–1941), Bengali poet, writer, composer

	and painter; author of *Gitanjali*; was awarded the Nobel Prize for Literature (1913)
Tartar	(also Tatar), Turkic speakers in west-central Russia, especially along the Volga River
Toda, Josei	(1900–58), the second president of Soka Gakkai, a direct disciple of the founding president, Tsunesaburo Makiguchi, and mentor of the third president, Daisaku Ikeda
Tokugawa shogunate	government by hereditary military dictator; a time of peace, political stability and economic growth in Japan from 1603–1867
Tolstoy, Lev N.	(1828–1910), Russian writer, one of the world's great novelists; representative works include *War and Peace* and *Anna Karenina*
Tower of Babel	a tower meant to reach God in heaven, described in Genesis 11:1–9; a myth inspired by a tower temple in Babylonia called "Babilu" (Gate of God)
Toynbee, Arnold J.	(1889–1975), English historian best known for his twelve-volume *A Study of History* (1934–61)
Trotsky, Leon	(1879–1940), Communist theorist and agitator, leader in the October Revolution, commissar of foreign affairs and war under Bolshevik rule, removed from power by Joseph Stalin
tsar	(also czar), Byzantine or Russian emperor
Turgenev, Ivan Sergeyevich	(1818–83), Russian novelist, poet and playwright known for topical, committed literature; representative work *Fathers and Sons*
Ukraine	country in southwestern Europe consisting of level plains and the Carpathian Mountains; heavy-industrial and mining-metallurgical complex, major producer of winter wheat and sugar beet
USSR	former republic that encompassed eleven time zones and had common boundaries with six European countries and six Asian countries; founded in 1917, dissolved in 1991
Valéry, Paul	(1871–1945), French poet, essayist and critic
veche	a popular assembly, a Russian institution

	from the 10th to the 15th centuries
velvet revolution	the end of the Czechoslovak communist regime in 1989
Vimalakirti	a wealthy Buddhist layman in the time of Shakyamuni; prototype of the ideal lay believer and protagonist of the Vimalakirti Sutra
Volga	the longest river in Europe and western Russia's principal waterway
Voronezh	a city in western Russia, and a center of the grain trade
Whitman, Walt	(1819–1892) US poet, journalist and essayist; author of *Leaves of Grass*
Yeltsin, Boris	(1931–), Russian politician, president of Russia (1990–99)
Zhukov, Marshal	(1896–1974), Soviet army commander in World War II, broke the siege in the Battle of Stalingrad

Index

abstract ideas, 85–96
Adygeans, 107
Afghanistan, 57
Africa, 86, 104, 150
Ainu, 142
Aitmatov, Chingiz, 13, 21–3, 100, 116, 160
Ajatashatru, 82, 160
Akutagawa, Ryunosuke, 47
Albert Schweitzer Prize, 132
Aleksandr II, Tsar, 100, 160
Altai, 107
America *see* United States of America
Angles, 90
anti-Semitism, 27, 85, 160
apathy, 24–5
Armenia, 96, 160
Aron, Raymond, 85
Asia, 68, 86, 92, 95, 104, 133
Asia-Pacific region, 56
Astaf'ev, Viktor Petrovich, 29
atheism, 112, 120, 126–7, 128, 129
Azerbaijan, 96, 160

Babeuf, François (Gracchus), 113, 117
Babouvists, 115, 116
Bakunin, Mikhail, 139
Balkan Peninsula, 73, 150, 160, *see also* names of countries
Balkars, 97
Baltic nations, 89
Bashkirs, 107
Belarus, 11, 160
Belavezheskaja forests, 11
Belinsky, Vissarion Grigoryevich, 8, 99, 160
Belov, Vasily, 29
Belovezh Agreement, 49, 87, 91, 160
Berdyaev, Nikolai, 30, 48, 137, 160
  on abstract politics, 91
  on Christianity and Communism, 69–70

on ideology of sacrifice, 37
on importance of spirituality, 126
on Lenin's attitude to religion, 75
on national identity, 101
on religious faith, 77–8
on universalism, 86–7, 104
Bergson, Henri, 47, 160
Berlin University, 99
Berlin Wall, fall of, 153
Bernstein, Eduard, 121
betrayal, 60
Bible, 126, *see also* Matthew; New Testament; Old Testament
Bimbisara, King, 82, 161
Bismarck, Otto von, 86
Bloom, Allan: *The Closing of the American Mind*, 127–8
bodhisattvas, 82–3
Boken Shonen (Boy's Adventures) (magazine), 9
Bolsheviks/Bolshevism, 2–3, 4, 19, 28, 44, 48, 55, 91, 92, 100, 101, 112, 117, 119, 125, 134, 139, 141, 161
Bosnia, 149–50, 151, 159
Bosnian Serbs, 149, 150
Brezhnev, Leonid, 25, 29
British empire, 89
Brzezinski, Zbigniew, 161
  The Grand Failure: The Birth and Death of Communism in the 20th Century, 101
Buddha, 3–4, 71–2, 82, 108
Buddha nature, 84, 141
Buddhism,
  and Christianity, 70–1
  Ikeda's acceptance of, 6–7
  and Japanese syncretism, 76
  and religious conflict, 73
  and Russians, 131
  teachings and ideas, 3–4, 7, 8, 34, 40, 53, 70–2, 82–3, 84, 116, 130, 137–8, 139, 140–1, 158